THE INSTAGRAM ICEBERG

THE INSTAGRAM ICEBERG

CHANGING THE WAY WE THINK ABOUT INSTAGRAM AS A BUSINESS TOOL

MOLLY BORMAN HEYMONT

NEW DEGREE PRESS

THE INSTAGRAM ICEBERG

Changing The Way We Think About Instagram As A Business Tool

ISBN

978-1-64137-544-3 *Paperback*

978-1-64137-545-0 *Kindle Ebook*

978-1-64137-546-7 *Digital Ebook*

For my son, Henry. We wrote this together.

CONTENTS

CHAPTER 1

THE INSTAGRAM ICEBERG

LARRY'S WIFE'S NIPPLES

Standing before 300 people in his Wharton School of Business class, Larry Heymont grabbed the mic, took a deep breath, and announced, "I'm here to talk about my wife's nipples."

The crowd went wild and relief washed over Larry's face. Understandably, Larry had some concerns about addressing his wife's nipples in front of his classmates, as nipples–or any part of the female anatomy for that matter–were not in the typical rotation of publicly discussed business school topics, especially at a school-sanctioned event.

Startups, valuations, and growth hacking? Yes. All day long!

Nipples? No. Never.

But, as Larry continued his speech, it became clear his wife's nipples had more in common with the business world than anyone would have initially suspected.

Larry's wife's nipples, or more accurately, *my* nipples, have been at the forefront of all my major business decisions for the last four years. My company, Just Nips, makes adhesive nipple enhancers for women who want that extra "chilly" look.

The product itself is an adhesive petal-shaped pasty, not unlike the ones women wear to cover up their nipples. Instead, Just Nips pasties feature a soft plastic nipple shape on top that, when worn underneath your shirt, look like a fully erect nipple.

Our customers range from women wearing Just Nips for cosmetic reasons to women who use our product as a nipple replacement after undergoing a non-nipple-sparing mastectomy.

From a business perspective, Just Nips has been fully profitable since our second month in production and we have been the fastest growing breast cancer accessory on the market for two years in a row.

Reporters, panelists, and fellow entrepreneurs often ask me how I've managed to scale Just Nips so big and so fast, and my answer always comes as a shock: I haven't spent any of my precious time, energy, or company resources on Instagram in the past few years.

Of course, this wasn't always the case.

SOME BACKGROUND

Before I started Just Nips, I was busy building my career in social media. I got my "big break," if you will, in 2013 while working as a copywriter for Ralph Lauren. On my way to work one morning, my neighbor Josh grabbed my phone and added himself to my list of Instagram followers. I didn't think much of it, except for the fact that I was late for work, and he wouldn't let go of my phone. Annoyed, I grabbed my phone back and left for the day. I noticed later that Josh posted on Instagram all day long. And he was funny. *And* he had a ton of followers. I was intrigued.

The next time I ran into Josh, we talked about his account, @TheFatJewish (today boasting over eleven million followers), and how he and his then-wife were also running separate Instagram accounts for their dogs. It's important to note that in 2013, we definitely weren't referring to specific Instagram profiles as "accounts"–this was a time way before people had multiple profiles, business profiles or "finsta" profiles. In fact, you couldn't even toggle between profiles like you can today. You had to manually log out and log back in each time you wanted to post. What a pain!

These were the early years. What Josh and his then-wife were doing, essentially building up their personal brands (a.k.a. pioneering the influencer concept) and their dogs' brands (creating an entire ecosystem of pet influencers), was uncharted territory. From what I could tell, they were also making good money.

I was soon brought on board to help run their dogs' Instagram accounts–a new side gig I could manage alongside my desk job at Ralph Lauren. As needed, I would take the dogs to "meetings" like photoshoots and appearances and capture content during my lunch break or free time, all while learning the ins and outs of this new Instagram economy.

After a while, I quit my job at RL and built up a roster of social media clients. I had quickly gotten the hang of juggling multiple clients with various goals and strategies when a dream opportunity came my way: to run social media for Barbara Corcoran, the real estate mogul turned *Shark Tank* star. I had relentlessly emailed her team until I got the interview and was hired on the spot.

It goes without saying that working for Barb was very different than working with any of my other clients, mostly because her world was so unique. She wasn't just a single entity. Barbara's social media presence represented her, her personal business, and all of the businesses and entrepreneurs she invested in through *Shark Tank*. Barbara was extremely hands-on with the businesses she invested in on the show; therefore, I worked closely with those businesses. At this time, social media was all the rage, and figuring out how to "crack the code" and drive more Instagram-led sales for Barbara's portfolio companies was always top of mind.

In between posts, 'grams, and tweets, I found myself dreaming of running my own business. Given that watching *Shark Tank* for hours on end was a very real part of my new job description, I often found myself wondering why I couldn't do what the entrepreneurs pitching on my TV screen were doing. As far as I was concerned, I was in a unique position to make the leap into starting a product-based brand. I had e-commerce experience from Ralph Lauren, I had social media marketing experience from working with all of my clients, and surely some of Barbara's business expertise had rubbed off on me, right?

It was a fool-proof plan with the notable exception that I did not yet have a product to sell.

JUST NIPS

While cleaning out my desk drawer in my New York City apartment, I found a pack of pencil cap erasers you stick on the end of your pencils. I laughed to myself, thinking that they looked like pointy nipples. (Really mature!) Then, I found some safety pins and affixed the erasers to my bra where my real nipples are. I pulled a sweatshirt over my head and voila! I looked like the coldest girl in the world.

I began tinkering away, forming various shapes and sizes of erasers to correspond with various cold temperatures, and that was that–I finally had my product to sell. This momentary stroke of boredom (read: genius) would serve as my foray into entrepreneurialism.

I spent a few months getting everything together–from the scary stuff, like engineering and manufacturing, to the boring work, like legal necessities and payroll, to the fun part of branding and marketing. Just Nips Fake Nipples, designed to make you look cold and feel hot, was officially born.

In 2016, one of my first consumer-facing steps was to start the Just Nips Instagram account to promote the lifestyle of what it means to have "cold" nipples. This was fitting, considering I had worked in social media for many years, running accounts for multiple brands. I was excited to go back to focusing on what I was good at, which was building an online community.

From a best-practices standpoint, my Just Nips social media strategy followed the playbook. I maintained the perfect mix of staged product photography, user generated content, relevant memes, and pop culture images. I had video content and splashy graphics. I had a carefully curated vibe full of pinks, creamy whites, and navy (our brand colors) with copy to match. The captions were the ideal balance of informative and funny. My follower count kept growing and growing.

When Just Nips received positive or negative press (FYI, if you start a nipple company, you're going to get some negative press, even if your core business is social-impact-related), our Instagram follower count would skyrocket, and we would get an influx of orders on our website.

After a few months, the business was profitable. And once it was profitable, I knew I wanted to allocate some of the profits toward an Instagram advertising campaign that I assumed would be the holy grail of all ad campaigns known to mankind. Why? Because so far, everything else was working beautifully on the social media front. After all, people paid me to do this on their behalf. I was an expert with the Midas touch!

Naively, I figured that anyone who is anyone (specifically my potential new customers) lives on Instagram, scrolling with a credit card in hand. Even more, Just Nips checks all the boxes a millennial-focused brand needs to check, like having a catchy name (check!), a memorable product (check!), and ties to a social-impact initiative (did I mention the Just Nips' breast cancer donation program? Check!).

I would soon learn that my hero's journey was beginning to run its course. I wasn't generating the Insta-traffic I had expected. I wasn't gaining followers like I used to. I wasn't getting the likes and comments I had in the beginning. My ads weren't working.

Something was wrong.

After doubting Instagram as a business tool for some time and feeling like I was the only one who couldn't get it right, I looked to other brands to see how I could emulate their best practices, but I still couldn't find my way.

My dreams of turning Just Nips into the Warby Parker of Nipples, the Glossier of Nipples, or the Uber of Nipples were slowly fading away. I sought out other consultants, experts, and online courses to understand where I could've possibly gone wrong. *I must get these ads to work*, I thought to myself.

I wasted tons of time and money trying to crack the code, even though the secret was right in front of me the entire time: *Could it be that Instagram isn't the magic elixir business tool we hype it up to be?*

THE SAGA CONTINUES

Before I could reach any real conclusions on my own, Instagram made the choice for me and kicked Just Nips off of the platform. To many Just Nips customers, our product is a breast cancer accessory. According to Instagram, however, Just Nips might as well have been a hardcore pornography account, as the platform's policies prohibit the female nipple to be featured in any manner.

I was frustrated, to say the least. Up until this point, I'd relied on an Instagram-first marketing strategy. This was 2016, and using Instagram for business was all the rage. Scroll through *Forbes, Entrepreneur,* and *Inc's* websites on any given day, and you were bound to come across article after article about some new product hitting the million-dollar mark during Q1 with Instagram ads alone, expert analysis on how to best optimize Instagram for your company, and how easy it was to become the next big Instagram-based business. In my own network of entrepreneurs, all everyone could talk about was their Instagram strategy, ad spend, and content optimization.

Once Just Nips was kicked off of Instagram, I was faced with a difficult decision: I could either shut the company down completely or figure out a way to exist as a business in the Instagram Era without using Instagram. While the former seems dramatic, at the time it felt like a viable possibility.

Ultimately, I decided to get over the Insta-drama and scale my business without it.

MOVING ON

When I let go of Instagram and focused on the real meat and potatoes of running my company, I realized how shortsighted I'd been to have ever thought Instagram could provide the returns our other strategies were yielding at the same cost. Minimal press efforts and a first stab at an email strategy carried Just Nips to its first one-thousand-order day. To think that with more traditional outreach I could continue to grow the business was the only proof of concept I needed to walk away from Instagram once and for all.

Instead of Instagram marketing, I focused on other areas where I could shine–like offline, old-fashioned community building (yes, face-to-face interactions!), collaborations, PR, speaking engagements, a direct mail strategy, and a growing email list.

While I was initially hesitant to talk about how my company was not using Instagram as a primary marketing resource, I was eventually shouting it from the rooftops to anyone who would listen. People looked at me like I was crazy, especially at entrepreneur meetups and panels. But when I explained how much our conversion rates and overall sales increased once I stopped using the platform exclusively, it hit home hard.

Years and many, many iterations of Instagram's advertising policies later, I'm finding that more and more entrepreneurs are looking to me for advice on how to move beyond their reliance on Instagram.

In entrepreneurial circles, ditching Instagram is steadily gaining momentum. However, to understand the magnitude of this shift, it's important to note the extent to which most businesses have relied on the platform.

INSTAGRAM AS A BUSINESS TOOL

Over one billion people use Instagram every single month, with half of them scrolling through the platform every day. On average, it's reported that people spend fifty-three minutes per day on the app.[1] The sheer volume of reachable consumers on the platform, combined with Instagram's hyper-targeting capabilities, positions the app as the ideal tool for businesses to connect and sell to their desired demographic. Oh, and as a bonus, Instagram is free and relatively simple to use.

1 Molla, Rani. Wagner, Kurt. "People spend almost as much time on Instagram as they do on Facebook." Vox.com. https://www.vox.com/2018/6/25/17501224/instagram-facebook-snapchat-time-spent-growth-data. (accessed January 26, 2020).

After acquiring Instagram in 2012, Facebook has prioritized its darling. Following the acquisition, Instagram has grown to become one of Facebook's primary revenue verticals, thanks to the app's robust advertising capabilities and appeal to business owners hoping to broaden their audience.

The facts speak for themselves. According to Instagram:

- Of the over 500 million daily active users, over 220 million Instagram users visit at least one business profile each day.
- Incredibly, over twenty-five million businesses use Instagram for customer acquisition and general awareness (read: marketing).
- Two-thirds of business profile visits come from people who aren't already following that business.
- With one in three small businesses on Instagram saying they built their business on Instagram, the platform has become its own self-sustaining economy.

It's hard to ignore the magnitude of Instagram's presence and easy to see the appeal of starting an account for your business. In the startup space, Instagram has been touted as the be-all and end-all for starting and running a business, because businesses know that's where customers are likely to be. Instagram is also frequently praised for being the best, most efficient, and most cost-effective way to scale customer acquisition efforts, brand exposure, and sales in a short timeframe.

However, conversations with business owners who rely on the platform on a daily basis have revealed that this is not at all the case.

Businesses both big and small are growing frustrated with the rising costs to post and run ads on Instagram. At the same time, companies buying advertisements on the platform today are yielding diminishing returns from their invested ad spend, especially in the last few years. To add insult to injury, Instagram has a reputation for having a finicky backend for business users, while its consumer-facing frontend has also experienced a record-high number of outages over the last year. All of these factors are simply catastrophic for brands relying on the platform to hit sales goals.

So, what's a brand to do when Instagram turns out *not* to be the business darling it was expected it to be? Hopefully, that's why you picked up this book! In this book:

- I explore case studies on some of the most notable companies that paved the way for the rest of us in demonstrating how Instagram could be optimized for business in the first place.
- I speak with entrepreneurs who are growing frustrated with the rising cost of using Instagram and are debating what to do next.
- I interview entrepreneurs who have seen real-world success from properly utilizing Instagram. Spoiler alert: their successes have a lot to do with how they operate offline.

- I explore what's next for businesses and what you can do to get ahead of the curve, beating the rush before your competition catches on.

Additionally, you will:

- Understand how the Insta-landscape has evolved since its conception, how these monumental shifts affect business accounts and personal accounts, and what this means for you.
- Hear from various founders who share their insights regarding the highs and lows of entrepreneurialism in the Instagram age.
- Learn about the increasing interest in offline customer acquisition methods from the brands who are doing it best.
- Learn new marketing strategies that enable your business to thrive without a dependence on a singular business tool.
- Most importantly, be able to apply the tactical strategies learned here to *your* business.

The Instagram Iceberg is for those who are willing to zig while the rest of the world zags. Let's go!

CHAPTER 2

THE ICEBERG THEORY

HEMINGWAY, MEET INSTAGRAM

The title of this book, *The Instagram Iceberg*, is a modern tribute to Ernest Hemingway's Iceberg Theory. When writing fiction (and critiquing others' fiction), Hemingway was a staunch believer in elimination. His Iceberg Theory, also known as the Theory of Omission,[2] states that the true quality of a piece could only be judged by the quality of material *left out*. In other words, Hemingway believed that the more details you leave out, the more powerful your story becomes.

What you see on the surface pales in comparison to what is invisible underneath.

And Instagram is one gigantic iceberg.

2 "Wikipedia: Iceberg Theory," Wikimedia Foundation, last modified December 18, 2019, 09:25, https://en.wikipedia.org/wiki/Iceberg_theory.

From the platform itself to each individual account, there is more to the shiny, visible parts of Instagram than meets the eye. The invisible parts–from the number of takes it took to get that candid-looking wedding photo just right, to the amount of money poured into staging the perfect new product announcement–are far more indicative of the real story (and cost!) than what the photograph, its caption, likes, and comments will ever reveal.

For those using Instagram to promote their business, the instant ability to see what other brands are doing, whether it be your direct competition or other Insta-veteran companies, is a double-edged sword. On one hand, you can look to entrepreneurs and brands you admire for inspiration and best practices. On the other hand, you can get stuck in the frustrating trap of believing that what you see on Instagram is exactly as it appears.

Because followers don't know what goes on behind the scenes of each post, we may readily dismiss all the hard work and non-Instagram-focused businesses initiatives as nonexistent and internalize the made-for-Instagram moments as the full picture.

This is the Instagram Iceberg.

As brands strive to become like people and people curate their personal content to appear more like a brand, the lines blur even more. Intellectually, we know to never trust brands like we would a best friend, but when a carpet company speaks to you in the same familiar tone that you and your bestie from middle school have conversed in for years, a subconscious layer of trust is formed. And as for the carpet company, that's exactly what it is going for. Even more, the Instagram algorithm is conditioned to serve us content similar to what we already like, have searched for in the past, and (increasingly) are currently talking about.

If you "like" a picture from a certain brand shot in a certain style, you will be shown more of that same style of content. Think of it as a digital confirmation bias, in that certain posts, products, and even influencers appear to be more popular, not because they necessarily *are* but because we see them all the time. From the Instagram user's perspective, this creates an echo chamber and reinforces the idea that what we see must be working for these businesses in some capacity. The Instagram algorithm inherently grants a false sense of legitimacy to people, products, and brands that may not necessarily deserve it.

As a recreational Instagram user, it's easier to understand the fact that posts from people in our real lives are just the tip of the iceberg, and yes, couples who post make-out pictures with gushing captions all day long might not be (read: are definitely *not*) that happy in real life. And we know deep down that, despite what the picture may look like, not everyone was smiling ear-to-ear that entire night at the party. We know this because we know the people behind the posts. We see them during their ups and downs and can recognize that their Instagram feed is just a highlight reel of their real lives.

So why is it so hard for Instagram users to realize that these same truths apply to businesses?

- That yes, the most successful brands on Instagram aren't necessarily the most profitable or, oftentimes, even close to profitable at all.
- And those co-founders posting from their yacht-themed work retreat off the coast of Ibiza might not know how they're going to pay their suppliers next month.
- And that brand you love so much, with the seemingly super high engagement on every single post is just as frustrated as you are with the dismal returns on their Instagram ads.

Because we aren't applying the Iceberg Theory to every post we see when we, as business owners or casual Instagram users, mindlessly scroll through the 'Gram during our lunch break or for longer than we'd like to admit on weekends.

THE ICEBERG ILLUSION

Oftentimes, people look to Instagram as a magic elixir to solve their business woes with the mindset that if you can just get a few more followers, you will have the public renown you crave *and* the corresponding profits.

But the relationship between followers, likes, and sales is not–I repeat, *NOT*–a one-to-one (to-one) direct correlation. It is very possible for a post to garner fifty thousand likes and not generate a single sale. In fact, this is often the case.

One of the main reasons I believe business owners are so eager to make Instagram work is because we want it to be our one-stop-shop for customer acquisition. How amazing would that be? With an unprecedented amount of data and analytics available at our fingertips, knowing our customers are just a few taps away, the convenience of Instagram for business is understandably appealing.

We've heard the success stories of the unicorn businesses that put some money here and there into Instagram and watched the sales rolled in. We've seen the press about brands who have cracked the code, and we wonder, "why not me?"

Having been in your shoes before, I know firsthand how easy it is to fall victim to this false narrative. When it comes to using Instagram for your business, the first step is recognizing that what we see on Instagram is an iceberg illusion. Cue Celine Dion and the Titanic theme song!

We must understand that followers and likes are a social construct, not a business metric. Similarly, the disparity between Insta-fame and profit is huge. A large Instagram following does not directly correspond to business success, even though on the surface, at the tip of the iceberg, it may appear to.

CHAPTER 3

THE DIRECT-TO-CONSUMER LANDSCAPE

BACK TO SCHOOL

"Shut the fuck up about Warby fucking Parker!" –Me, many times throughout 2017.

I never technically enrolled in business school but ended up going anyway. About one year after I started Just Nips, my husband Larry let me know we were officially moving to Philadelphia so he could join the Wharton School of Business, Class of 2019.

Though his acceptance ranks as one of the best days of his life, to me, our impending move from New York City to Philadelphia felt like a devastating blow to all the work I had done over the last year. How could I possibly relocate without disrupting my business? The one I spent every waking minute of the last year building, perfecting, and finally feeling confident about?

Larry tried to sell me on the positives and reiterated how tons of great startups had come out of Wharton in the last decade, most notably the billion-dollar eyewear brand Warby Parker. He swore that being around like-minded entrepreneurs would be the best thing to ever happen to me and my business. Larry tried his best to convince me that his Wharton professors would be readily available to discuss my business, offer pearls of wisdom, explain eye-opening best practices, and introduce me to their extended networks and former students (perhaps even the legendary Warby Parker founders) who could help me learn from their entrepreneurial experiences.

So off to Philly we went, with a truck full of fake nipples in tow.

Upon arrival, one of the first things we did was attend a meeting for partners of students, people like me who were along for the ride while their spouses attended the program. At the meeting, I was given a badge that granted me access to a whole suite of amenities like the ability to attend Wharton-sponsored events, sit in on interesting classes, and perhaps most importantly, permission to use the printers to my heart's content. During this initial meeting, one of the mentors suggested that we (the partners) take full advantage of UPenn's renowned lecture series. The mentor went out of his way to explain that the founders of Warby Parker are Wharton MBA graduates and often come back to guest lecture a few times per year. "Trust me. You won't want to miss it!"

Throughout Larry's first semester, whenever I was out and about making new friends in my new city, someone would politely ask what I do for a living.

I would start my Just Nips spiel and someone would invariably bring up Warby Parker.

"You're like the Warby Parker of nipples!"

"You should talk to Adam Grant, the professor who advised the Warby Parker guys when they were MBA students!"

"You need to check out these slides about Warby Parker from my marketing class!"

I felt like I had been inducted into a Warby Parker fan club that I never signed up for. All anyone wanted to talk about was Warby fucking Parker!

The truth is, I didn't get it. I didn't yet understand why Warby Parker was significant enough to warrant this much airtime from seemingly everyone in the city of Philadelphia. Sure, I knew that Warby Parker was a huge, game-changing, billion-dollar business, and that the founders got their start at Wharton. That part was crystal clear. However, I did not fully grasp the extent to which Warby Parker pioneered the direct-to-consumer model and ultimately paved the way for the consumer goods space we find ourselves in today.

THE DIRECT-TO-CONSUMER MODEL

Warby Parker is credited with bringing the direct-to-consumer model into the mainstream with its buy-online, try-on-at-home eyeglasses. This sales framework was revolutionary for many reasons.

For starters, buying eyeglasses online without first trying them on was unheard of in 2010. Who would feel comfortable shopping like this? It turned out, millions of people would... and they would rave about the experience.

Second, Warby Parker disrupted a partial manufacturing monopoly that had been holding the world's most prominent eyewear brands hostage for decades.

Pre-Warby, Luxottica was the one main eyeglass conglomerate responsible for pretty much every pair of glasses you'd ever come across. In 2014, Luxottica controlled 80 percent of the major brands in the twenty-eight-billion-dollar global eyeglasses industry.[3]

This little-known eyewear manufacturer was wildly profitable, producing and designing frames for companies from Ray-Ban and Oakley to Prada and Chanel and just about any brand in between, including the ill-fated Google Glass. As of 2014, Luxottica estimated that at any given point in time, over half

3 Swanson, Ana. "Meet the Four-Eyed, Eight-Tentacled Monopoly That is Making Your Glasses So Expensive." Forbes.com https://www.forbes.com/sites/anaswanson/2014/09/10/meet-the-four-eyed-eight-tentacled-monopoly-that-is-making-your-glasses-so-expensive/#765283746b66 (January 26, 2020)

a billion people around the world were wearing its glasses. If a brand had previously wanted to expand into eyewear, it would head straight to Luxottica and have the company handle the manufacturing. In turn, Luxottica would send the brand a finished product with the brand's logo stamped on the side of each pair of frames and then bill the brand accordingly.

Luxottica had little competition, which also meant that it could have complete control over how much glasses cost. Since it had a near monopoly on the eyeglasses market, pricing was always in its favor. Luxottica's position in the eyeglass industry allowed it to set the prices of "its goods near the highest amount that consumers would be willing to pay for them, unlike more competitive industries, in which competition both encourages constant innovation and forces the price of goods down toward what they cost to manufacture."[4]

Warby Parker aspired to offer consumers a reasonably priced alternative. Instead of designing a few pairs of trendy eyeglasses and contracting Luxottica to manufacture the frames, Warby implemented a modern vertical integration model by bringing manufacturing in-house. Vertical integration is key to keeping costs down and enabled Warby Parker to provide its consumers with what would have been $500 eyeglasses (if they had worked with Luxottica) at one-fifth of the price.

---

4 Swanson, Ana. "Meet the Four-Eyed, Eight-Tentacled Monopoly That is Making Your Glasses So Expensive.' Forbes.com https://www.forbes.com/sites/anaswanson/2014/09/10/meet-the-four-eyed-eight-tentacled-monopoly-that-is-making-your-glasses-so-expensive/#765283746b66 (January 26, 2020)

Warby Parker successfully removed the manufacturing middleman from its supply chain and set out to further reduce its costs by exclusively selling its glasses online, thus bypassing wholesalers and their built-in commissions. Instead of coming across Warby Parker glasses in a retail store, customers would find out about Warby Parker directly from Warby Parker, hence the business practice's aptly titled "direct-to-consumer" model.

In its purest form, the digitally native direct-to-consumer model removes all of the expensive middlemen (e.g., manufacturers, wholesalers, retailers, landlords, etc.), which can be significant barriers to entry for cash-strapped entrepreneurs. In this sense, the direct-to-consumer model allows more brands the freedom to sell their product their way.

Warby Parker realized its model's value proposition: that nothing stands between a brand and its customers anymore. No longer could wholesale vendors or mercurial department store buyers pull the rug out from under a brand. No longer did a brand need to sign a ten-year lease on its first retail store before knowing if people were even interested in the product. Middlemen no longer took a cut of a brand's hard-earned profits.

Viewed through the lens of Warby Parker, your business is just you, your supply chain and your customers.

Without anyone standing in its way, Warby Parker revolutionized how companies are able to interact with their customers. Instead of hoping your wholesale partners will represent you the way you want to be represented, you have complete control over communication with the very people buying your product. You can control the messaging. And most importantly, you know exactly who your customer is–you have their contact information readily available and can check in to see if they're satisfied with their purchase or, better yet, keep them apprised of upcoming promotions in hopes of persuading them to become a repeat customer.

The Warby Parker model changed the way we think about building businesses today and inspired an onslaught of cross-industry copycats—the Warby Parker of mattresses, the Warby Parker of lingerie, and my personal favorite, the Warby Parker of nipples.

A NEW MIDDLEMAN

The direct-to-consumer model–combined with a heavy dose of modern technology that allows new companies to operate as digitally native entities–has successfully enabled brands to enter the consumer products industry sans the traditional middlemen like manufacturers, wholesalers, and a retail presence.

By removing some of the previous biggest barriers to entry for startups, Warby Parker opened the floodgates for thousands of new companies, across hundreds of industries, to join in on the fun.

But doing this also made room for a new middleman to take its place:

Instagram.

A business's manufacturers and wholesale partners previously gave it credibility, whereas consumers now look to follower counts and Instagram presence to determine a brand's validity. In the days before Instagram, a startup would also be inclined to hire a PR team and seasoned marketers to spread the word about its launch.[5]

With the goal of being as literal as possible with the "direct-to-consumer" method, as well as the cultural inclination for startups to disrupt all the ways of the past, why not also cut marketing and PR costs and use the seemingly cost-free Instagram platform to promote your business and message? Everyone in the startup world seemed to have the same idea at the same time.

Instagram, in turn, capitalized on this mass migration to its platform and began charging more for ads, making it harder for businesses to grow followings and organically earn highly-coveted reach. Instagram encouraged businesses to run advertisements and utilize pay-to-play strategies that fuel growth.

---

5 Warby Parker utilized a robust multi-pronged PR and marketing strategy, but the success of the direct-to-consumer model that they pioneered led many brands to want to keep cutting out more seemingly superfluous players from the equation, like PR and marketing.

In other words, the more you pay Instagram to run your advertisements, the more people Instagram shows your ads to.

The more people who see your ads, the more people learn about your business.

The more people who learn about your business, the more people will buy your product.

In this scenario, the clear winner is Instagram, which is able to cash in on businesses that throw money at advertisements and are unwilling to see the platform for what it is: the new middleman.

SO NOW WHAT?

Much has changed in the ten years since Warby Parker's conception at the Wharton School of Business, and I can safely say that I now understand what the hype is all about (so much so, I wrote a book about it ... while wearing my Warby Parker frames).

Having said that, we are now in an environment where thousands of companies are using the same model and trying to do the same things.

In an effort to replicate the digitally native direct-to-consumer model that was so successful for Warby Parker, companies have trended toward an Instagram-reliant marketing strategy without realizing that they have willingly empowered a new gateway platform that now stands between them and their customers–Instagram itself.

The brands that best understand the role of this new and menacing middleman will be the ones left standing when the dust settles.

CHAPTER 4

HOW WE GOT HERE

IMPORTANT INFORMATION

While every business owner or advertiser has the ability to choose to advertise on Instagram, Facebook, or both, for the purposes of this book, unless otherwise noted, I use Facebook and Instagram interchangeably, as the majority of advertisements are optimized to be shown on both platforms. And hey, sometimes I'll even throw in the phrase "social media advertisements" to spice it up. When I do, don't worry! I am still referencing Facebook and Instagram.

On a similar note, it goes without saying that Facebook has changed the way we communicate and paved the way for companies like Instagram to exist. However, the way I see it, Instagram as a visually driven platform and business tool is more nuanced than Facebook. If a picture tells a thousand words, an Instagram post tells one thousand, plus a caption. A Facebook post, with ads on the side and Messenger pop ups, does not pack the same punch.

When you hear about a new company for the first time, you're not checking its Facebook page to learn more. You're going straight to its Instagram profile. From its profile, you learn about the company from a 3x3 grid and gain an acute understanding of exactly how many other people are interested in the brand from its follower count. In one glance, you know everything you need to know to formulate precisely how you feel about the brand.

The same principles apply to an Instagram ad for a brand you've never heard of. You can immediately view a snapshot of said brand's Instagram profile and decide to proceed with the purchase or not. One of the driving forces behind my research of this topic was how different my shopping and ad-clicking behavior is on Facebook versus Instagram. I found that, overall, I respond far better to Instagram ads presented to me in a bright and splashy manner–sandwiched between pictures of my best friends' dogs and my former coworkers–than I do a Facebook ad immediately following a peculiar news article that popped up because someone I friended ten years ago commented on it. Though you could make the case here that I am more drawn to relevancy, I believe it's the visual aspect that really gets me to follow through and click on the ad.

The more I researched, the more I found that when brands reported their digital ad spend (if they were willing to report their ad spend at all, which is a different topic altogether), they grouped Facebook and Instagram expenditure together. This makes sense, as you need to use the Facebook portal to run an

Instagram ad campaign, and it all gets billed as one lump sum. I found it difficult to get true numbers on Instagram-only spend and I realized that this was not a roadblock, but an interesting glimpse into the way Facebook and Instagram operate today. It seems to me that right now, the cultural phenomenon that is Instagram plays a more forward-facing role in business decisions than Facebook, which lays low but is still heavily involved, especially in advertising. We just don't talk about it as much.

Regardless, when it came time to choose a title for this book, *The Instagram Iceberg* sounded way better than *The Facebook and Instagram Iceberg*. Hopefully that cleared up any lingering questions you might have had, if you have even gotten so far as to consider them at this point.

HOW WE GOT HERE

When you first downloaded the Instagram app, you probably never envisioned future you reading a self-help book on how to successfully untie yourself from the platform's grasp.

But here we are!

In 2010, Instagram launched as a photo filtering and sharing app without an advertiser in sight. When Facebook's acquisition of Instagram was announced in 2012, many were quick to note that ads would be on their way any minute now, as ads were Facebook's primary means of generating revenue at the time.

Instagram did gradually roll out ads, first only offering the service to certain companies before making them available to virtually any person with a Facebook account and a credit card. Today, we are looking at over two million advertisers on Instagram, a number that grows by the day.[6]

An influx of ads to the platform–combined with the removal of Instagram's chronological feed– disrupted what I and many entrepreneurs using the platform at the time call Instagram's Golden Age.

When we look back on the Golden Age of Instagram, specifically the Insta-era between 2013-2014, what we remember is part truth and part urban legend. And as is often true with urban legends in any capacity, the elements of Instagram folklore we cling to most tightly have been grossly exaggerated as time goes on.

THE URBAN LEGEND: INSTAGRAM'S GOLDEN AGE

In its simplest terms, the Golden Age of using Instagram for business was a time when all it took was an idea and a few pictures to get going–when good ideas supported by even better content could go viral based on merit and merit alone.

Then Instagram introduced advertising options, and they were dirt cheap compared to the traditional methods of ad buying. Would you have rather spent a minimum of $500,000

---

6 Instagram. "Stand Out with Instagram." Instagram.com. https://business.instagram.com/getting-started/ (accessed January 26, 2020).

for an ad buy in Vogue (while shelling out thousands more for an advertising agency to create your campaign) or pay $5/day on Instagram (a platform that's otherwise free) with the added bonus of real-time data about how many people your ad reaches, where they are located, and if they ultimately click "buy"? The choice was simple.

For consumers, being on the platform during Instagram's Golden Age was addicting (and still is.) Having the ability to find shiny new products that no one else had and bring these new, exciting brands to your personal network was always a thrill. Social capital was there for the taking!

As for entrepreneurs, everyone saw opportunity. New brands and products flooded the platform every single day.

If you wanted to be an entrepreneur with an Instagram-only marketing strategy during the Golden Age, legend has it that this process was a fairly simple one. You would decide to be the next big thing in say, the toothbrush industry, banking on the idea that the digitally native direct-to-consumer model was the best path forward, and any and every market can and should be challenged, disrupted, and brought into the future. You would make some pre-manufacturing tweaks to streamline the familiar product design, making it thinner, sleeker, and cooler, while coming up with a few splashy brand colors that would be all over your website and, of course, the toothbrushes themselves. You would conceptualize the perfect name for your new company, too–one that practically guarantees success thanks to the way it fuses just the right amount of brand clarity with a hint of irony.

And just like that, your startup TEETHbrshs is born. By the time your first purchase order came in from China, you are all set up with an online shop and ready to sell.

You take the product to your personal Facebook page to get the ball rolling, post a few pictures and tell your existing network, comprised of friends, family, and people you haven't seen since high school about your new business and watch as your network begins shopping on your site in droves. Oh, and while you are packing and shipping out TEETHbrshs from your parents' garage, you remind everyone to also follow your new company on Instagram.

You take the profits from your initial sales and put them straight into Facebook and Instagram ads. Get a sale, make an ad. Get a sale, make an ad. Connect with some influencers who will post videos raving about your product, brushing their teeth with your TEETHbrshs gift set (you make gift sets now, too) morning and night and watch your new brand loyalists pour in. Repeat, repeat, repeat, scale, scale, scale until TEETHbrshs' Instagram page has hundreds of thousands of followers, is insanely profitable, and you're doing the press circuit, seeing your face all over *Forbes*, *Business Insider,* and the like.

You did it. You followed the tried-and-true, direct-to-consumer business model of the digital age and are now the Warby Parker of toothbrushes, the Casper mattress of toothbrushes, the Away luggage of toothbrushes. What's your secret? Instagram ads.

THE REALITY OF THE SITUATION

The issue is, this version of being a business owner on Instagram is simply not true. It's a mirage. It wasn't *totally* true during Instagram's Golden Age, and it certainly isn't true today.

This glorified version of Instagram entrepreneurialism is a story we've heard time and time again and, as entrepreneurs, we are eager to replicate the model for our own businesses. If all it takes are some pretty, high-resolution photographs of your made-in-China product and some ad spend, how hard could it be?

For anyone who has dabbled in entrepreneurialism in the past, you know you need more than an Instagram account to find and gain customers' trust, which is the precursor to convincing them to click "buy." In 2020, a robust content strategy and Instagram ads alone do not guarantee a profitable business.

You know, deep down, this version of success seems too good to be true—because it is. So, why do we hear this veneer of a story time and time again? Why are we fed the same narrative about the impact of using Instagram for business if it's simply not true? Because we aren't listening to the rest of the story.

DEATH OF THE GOLDEN AGE

In 2016, when Instagram changed things up–making everyone's feeds "more relevant" (Mark Zuckerberg's words) as opposed to what we were used to seeing, which was posts in chronological order–the outcry was global, and it was loud. People were upset. Visibility and likes went down for the average user and "Insta-preneur." It was a very dramatic time for everyone involved.

The change also exposed another side of Instagram that users were reluctant to accept: the algorithm. Instagram's algorithm determines what you see on your feed and when you see it. The algorithm consists of dynamic lines of code that organize content for you based on what it "thinks" you want to see first. It can be understood as the ultimate pain point for entrepreneurs who rely on the platform as well as for digital marketers who are expected to understand this mysterious entity, because the performance of certain posts over others has seemingly no rhyme or reason.

Additionally, Facebook is intentionally tight-lipped on how the algorithm works, which is its prerogative, its intellectual property, and well within its rights to do, much to the dismay of its loyal users. Experts and users alike can offer nothing more than an educated guess on how the algorithm operates. However, a few things seem to be certain: birthdays, engagement announcements, gender reveals, and other milestone events are pushed to the top, whereas static product photography (what businesses rely on to showcase the products they are selling) is deemed less important.

As such, businesses have to go to extreme lengths to improve the quality of their content, (which gets pricey), and the competition for brands all vying for the same coveted spot is at an all-time high.

Changes to Instagram features, the ever-evolving algorithm, and increased competition mean that it is far more challenging for content to be seen by potential customers than it used to be, all contributing to the fact that Instagram is no longer the inexpensive marketing tool the Golden Age showcased it as.

THE GET-RICH-QUICK MENTALITY

So how did this narrative of "The Golden Age of Instagram," preaching that businesses can be successful with a heavy reliance on Instagram ads, get so ingrained in our minds and the entrepreneurial spirit? How come entrepreneurs, business owners, and venture capitalists often fall victim to the idea that Instagram ads and top-of-the-line content will solve all of our business woes and lead to sales, success, and riches?

For starters, the Golden Age mentality is a glorified "get rich quick" scheme optimized for the digital age. This mentality strips away some of the hardest and most time-consuming parts of running a business–like networking, dreaded cold calls, and cultivating relationships with prospective customers. Instead, it offers an easy way out by insisting the key to strong sales and organic growth is your online presence and Instagram advertising strategy.

Secondly, businesses and the media have a tendency to reference the same companies that *were* successful during this era time and time again. Collectively, we speak about the Golden Age like it's a broken record of direct-to-consumer's greatest hits. All but one of the entrepreneurs I interviewed for this book cited Glossier as the gold standard of direct-to-consumer brands who are currently killing it on Instagram. And most of the time, I didn't even have to ask a leading question like, "Which brand has the best social media presence?" Entrepreneurs were quick to point out who they wish to emulate on social early on in our conversations, which got me thinking: why?

CHAPTER 5

THE PERFECT STORM

EXPLORING THE LASTING LEGACY OF GLOSSIER

There is no doubt that Glossier, a digitally native direct-to-consumer cosmetics brand, is impressive.

When it started, Glossier offered a fresh take on the traditional cosmetics industry and disrupted it accordingly. Glossier went on from there to achieve cult-like status and is widely recognized as a pioneer of the direct-to-consumer method and social media marketing space.

For Glossier founder Emily Weiss, putting her company on Instagram was a no brainer. In a 2015 interview with *Entrepreneur*, she explains, "our customer is on Instagram, and it's how and where she's crafting her online persona, so we had to be there ... We used Instagram to launch Glossier, and that's really where the brand is taking shape."[7]

---

7 Davis, Grant. "How One Woman's Cosmetic Company 'Gramed Its Way to Insta-Success." Entrepreneur.com. https://www.entrepreneur.com/article/249328 (January 26, 2020).

There is no doubt Glossier benefited from starting during Instagram's formative years, or what I like to call the Golden Age. Emily's insistence on using Instagram–not just to promote her company, but to launch her company, and to later do research and development for her company–was brilliant. So much so that we're still talking about it today! It's hard to believe that Glossier was founded in 2014, over six years ago. Since then, Glossier's social media strategy has paved the way and normalized many of the marketing practices we see today on Instagram.

- For starters, Glossier is a leader in the content marketing space, pioneering the use of Instagram storytelling to make a bigger impact on its audience than traditional sales methods. Take for example what it means to have "dewy" skin, the look that started it all. Dewy skin gives off the impression that you are glowing from the inside out. You are healthy. You are happy. You are radiant. But, more often than not, the Glossier woman is busy—like, really busy, running around, checking things off her list, getting everything she has to get done, done. The Glossier woman isn't spending all day getting her glow on, but she still can look like it, right? After all, founder and CEO Emily Weiss has the dewy look and she is running a billion-dollar company. Surely, she isn't spending all day at the spa! But Glossier products can give you this aspirational look in five minutes or less. How do we know? Because that's the message behind Glossier's content marketing. And we all bought in.

- Glossier also mastered the art of communication with its customers. At a time when billion-dollar legacy brands told their consumers what products they needed and expected customers to blindly follow, Glossier flipped the model on its head by asking its core demographic exactly what products they needed and created a brand from there. For Glossier, customer service is not just giving customers an update on where their package is. Instead, it's a comprehensive communication strategy with an Instagram-heavy approach, including everything from responding to social media requests to conducting market research surveys through the app.

- Taking it one step further, Glossier has changed the game for what it means to build a brand by fostering a fiercely loyal community, a result of having constant communication with their customers.

- One look at any one of Glossier's more than forty products begs the question, "Which came first, the product or the art direction for its introductory Instagram post?" All of Glossier's products are picture-perfect, from their exterior packaging to their gooey insides, and both are ideal for Insta-content. Fast Company goes deeper, arguing, "its modern, minimalist packaging is designed to look good in photographs. Every Glossier product arrives in a reusable, pink plastic pouch that doubles as a handy

Instagram backdrop."[8] Not only are Glossier's products ideal for the brand's content, but the products also naturally make great content for you to create and share, too. Brilliant. Synergy at its finest.

- Since the beginning, every piece of Glossier's content has been on-brand in a revolutionary way, mostly due to the pressing need for so much content. The sheer volume of Instagram posts, stories and digital advertisements requires a serious amount of uniform marketing collateral, and Glossier has this mastered to a T. If you are even remotely familiar with Glossier and see an advertisement for the brand without any copy attached to it, the odds of you recognizing the ad is for Glossier are high. This directly corresponds to better conversation rates and higher performing ads. What more could a business want?

- Even the Insta-practice of "unboxing," or showing your network your latest purchase, was created largely as a response to the joy experienced upon receiving Glossier's pretty-in-pink packaging and adorable freebies.

- Speaking of ... what about the ubiquity of the color Millennial Pink, both on our screens and in real life? You can, of course, thank Glossier for starting and perpetuating the trend that seemingly won't go away.

---

8 Fast Company. "Most Innovative Companies." Fastcompany.com. https://www.fastcompany.com/company/glossier. (accessed January 26, 2020).

CLINGING TO THE PAST

Having any one of the above wins accredited to your brand is a huge feat, let alone all of them. But founders in our current landscape must realize that following in Emily's footsteps is a dated practice. The portion of Glossier's success fueled by Instagram cannot be replicated. If you were to copy Glossier's content strategy today, as many brands do, you would not have the same success, as many of these copycat brands do not.

Why? Because the digital landscape is entirely different today than it was in 2014. Previously tried-and-true tactics do not work in today's marketplace. And perhaps even more importantly, the consumer is entirely different than they were in 2014. Today's consumers are far savvier. They have completely different and much higher expectations of what they are willing to respond to online. They have greater choice, with millions of brands and accounts to explore on Instagram. They understand that when you opt in to follow a brand, you are bringing that brand into your life, among your closest friends and family, and you are choosing to interact with that brand most likely on a daily basis.

So, what does it mean when entrepreneurs are *still* talking about Glossier as the benchmark for great social? It means they are stuck in the past. Just like you would never rely on pen and paper to keep track of your sales leads today when far more sophisticated methods, like Salesforce, take into account not only the changing landscape but the savvier consumer as well, you should not rely on the Glossier playbook of social media for your brand in 2020.

THE 4-HOUR WORKWEEK

And then we have Tim Ferriss.

His iconic New York Times Bestseller *The 4-Hour Workweek* encapsulates the idea of the "set it and forget it" digital ad strategy. In his book, Tim argues that anyone with an Internet connection can free themselves from their 9-to-5 hellish existence and travel the globe while making more money than they could ever imagine just by setting up a good old-fashioned digital ad strategy. It's that simple!

Find a product (bonus: you don't even have to like that product–just make sure some other people do), set up a website, get a warehouse shipping and operations partner, create some digital ads, and watch the money roll in. Once your ads are set up, you don't even have to think about them anymore. Just sit back and watch your bank account grow by a couple of zeros week after week!

In his infamous book, Tim Ferriss lays out everything you need to do, step-by-step, to become filthy rich by taking advantage of inexpensive digital ad offerings. The problem is a lot, and I mean a *lot*, of people bought into this narrative, causing the entire system to come crashing down as the cost of digital ads began to soar in response to the demand. Of course, this is oversimplifying the problem a bit (getting into the details is what the rest of the book is for) and placing a lot of the blame on Tim (sorry, Tim), but his best-selling book paved the way for where we find ourselves today in the digital media landscape.

The 4-Hour Workweek came out in 2007, long before Instagram, mind you, and since then, advancements in technology have made starting your own online business easier than ever before. Today, actual companies make it their business to get *your* product made in China, with no knowledge of the Chinese or Mandarin languages required. You can create an online store in under ten minutes with easy-to-use Shopify templates. Don't like Shopify? Switch to one of its many competitors doing the same thing. You can get custom packaging made in under a week. You can lease space in a warehouse for your bulkiest products and outsource shipping with just a few clicks and maybe an introductory phone call. Need an office? Get a WeWork membership. Think business cards would help? Order them from Moo. Want a 1-800 number? Connect it to your cell phone. Need customers? Advertise to them online.

The easier it became to be an entrepreneur, the more competition across the board (specifically the internet) heated up. It's Supply and Demand 101. By the time Instagram rolled around, the Tim Ferriss dream, or a digitized version of the American Dream, was firmly cemented in our culture. And when Instagram launched ads, everyone who believed in what Tim was selling was quick to jump onboard.

The idea, the hope, and the dream of starting a company and relying on digital ads to find customers and make sales is now ingrained in our entrepreneurial mentality. We all want to be the internet millionaire who gets to explore the world on weekdays, all while checking in on our TEETHbrshs business just four hours a week. Who wouldn't? But the reality is that those days and the Instagram Golden Age are officially over.

The truth? Today's entrepreneurs need to employ other strategies to build their brands and sell their products. Many of these strategies are best utilized outside of the Instagram economy and away from the platform's constant hype. And I think at this point, even Tim Ferriss would agree!

CHAPTER 6

THE MARKETING FUNNEL

THE CONFETTI BAR

Is there anything better than those moments in life that call for a confetti shower? I think not!

And neither does Jessica Serra Huizenga, who woke up one morning and told her husband she wanted to open a confetti shop.

What's a confetti shop? A place where Jessica could design her own confetti, in various colors, shapes and sizes, while selling her bespoke designs to customers near and far.

Could a one-stop confetti shop really prove to be a profitable business? Believe it or not, Jessica learned that the answer is a resounding *yes*. People all over the world love confetti and live for those made-for-confetti moments. In the beginning,

Jessica began posting her custom confetti creations on Instagram and found it relatively easy to build a loyal fan base. This, of course, was a different time. In early 2014, the height of Instagram's Golden Age, organic growth on Instagram was still possible and businesses were not using the platform the way they are today.

Jessica posted photos of her unique confetti designs that she'd take on her iPhone, off the cuff and whenever she felt like it. She didn't adhere to a strict schedule. She didn't optimize her feed or post when industry professionals deemed it best. Jessica's organic approach to posting clearly resonated with customers and fans around the world, as she racked up thousands upon thousands of followers during her first few years on Instagram.

Jessica's story is similar to a lot of early adopters of Instagram who were out there hustling and creating in a world before content calendars and automated posting schedulers. She recounts building her business in the Golden Age: "When I first started, it was very much the early days and you didn't have to worry about the perfect lighting or anything like that. You would take a photo and post it and, you know, a million people liked it. People were excited and ready to consume content, and it was very easy to break into that world and just have people discover you, and people were seemingly more apt to share about it. [As a result, my business] grew very organically and very quickly."

In 2015, Jessica started to notice a shift and made business decisions accordingly. Instagram was becoming increasingly formal and more professional. Gone were the days of posting whatever, whenever. It's worth mentioning that at this time, Instagram was steadily ramping up its advertising options.

"We transitioned into posting very pretty and highly-curated photos–which is very different from when I first started and had no rhyme or reason for what or when I would post. As Instagram shifted, I became more aware of what time to post and what looked good and then we moved into the very over-planned and highly curated stage. At one time, I published three posts a day–morning, afternoon, and night. And the more I posted, the more each one did well, so it turned into this never-ending cycle that was so much work, but then things sort of flatlined and I went back to posting once per day."

From a business standpoint, it seemed like this new era of Instagram was increasingly time consuming, labor intensive, and expensive, yet Jessica's increased effort was not producing the desired results or driving the same social engagement as her earlier, less curated posts during Instagram's Golden Age.

As the years went by, Jessica, like so many founders who were early to adopt this type of Instagram-for-business model, became frustrated with the number of changes she had to make to yield the initial results to which she had become accustomed. Finally, she realized that Instagram was no longer her top sales driver: "We started to see a shift where just organic Google search was actually performing better. And then you know, Pinterest got in the mix. So now it's kind of a mix between Google organic search and Pinterest that are my top traffic drivers, with the caveat that I myself in the past year have started pulling back a little bit from Instagram, and I've just been trying to find my way back to a place that feels good. Because for a little bit there, it didn't really feel good anymore."

When the joy and social affirmation from posting charming images of confetti evaporates but this extra effort is growing your bottom line, that's one thing. But when it is miserable abiding by a set of curated posting norms that yield lackluster results, it's no wonder business owners like Jessica have become less reliant on Instagram for revenue growth and, oftentimes, flee the platform altogether.

Without realizing it, Jessica was using Instagram to drive her customers down the theoretical Marketing Funnel. She was able to find and retain a loyal audience who loved confetti as much as she did, convince them to shop her products and tell their friends about it, and these friends in turn would also shop her products and tell *their* friends about it. Jessica was inherently doing what marketing teams spend countless hours agonizing over, and she captured the very essence of what makes Instagram so alluring to businesses.

In today's Instagram economy, though, this behavior has proven more effective in theory than practice.

THE MARKETING FUNNEL

As easy as it appears to sell a product on Instagram, if you've picked up this book, you have probably either tried to post for your business on Instagram and found that orders were not coming in as expected, or you have a hunch that the platform isn't the sales tool it's cracked up to be.

When it comes to generating sales on Instagram, basic marketing principles still apply. And that's where the Marketing Funnel comes into play.

What exactly is the Marketing Funnel? If you've taken an introductory marketing class or hired someone in the field to help you with your digital ad strategy, you've no doubt heard about the Marketing Funnel (marketers love to talk about the funnel). The Marketing Funnel is the term that explains the ideal customer journey from the first time potential customers hear about the product (the top of the funnel) to when they finally click "shop" and then, ideally, when they tell their friends about how much they love their purchase, encouraging more people to go through the funnel themselves.

The Marketing Funnel involves five separate steps, start to finish:

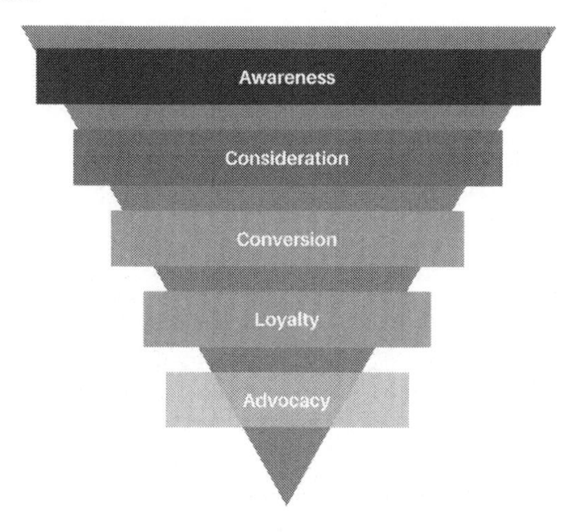

It goes without saying that the top of the funnel is the largest section, representing the broadest group of people you can reach within your market. As you continue down the funnel, each step becomes increasingly smaller as your pool of people who will ultimately turn into paying customers and advocates shrinks in size.

From a marketer's perspective, the beauty of Instagram is that you can hypothetically usher customers down all five funnel steps *within* the platform, something previously not possible with any other marketing strategy or on any other shopping platform.

Consider this: before social media or the internet, a customer journey could start at the **awareness** stage when they see a commercial for your product on tv.

Then, that potential customer has to make their way into your store or a store that sells your product to learn more in the **consideration** stage.

Then, that same potential customer has to decide to purchase on the spot or come back another time, leading to **conversion.**

Then, that customer has to be so blown away by the product that he or she vows to be a **loyal** customer for life.

Then, to **advocate** for your brand, that customer has to run into his or her friend who is also in the market for a similar item, and the initial customer has to encourage this friend to shop your product.

That's a lot of effort. In fact, too much effort. Too much time passes between the top of the funnel and the bottom. Too much is left to chance in this traditional Marketing Funnel.

So, when Instagram initially came out and had the ability to link to your website in your bio where customers can shop within minutes (even seconds) of hearing about your brand for the first time, it seemed too good to be true.

THE INSTAGRAM MARKETING FUNNEL

The Instagram Marketing Funnel is a far more efficient version of the traditional funnel. Each step looks like this:

- The **awareness** step represents the first time your potential customer is introduced to your brand. On Instagram, this may be a result of automatic discovery from the Discovery page itself, aimless scrolling, or perhaps seeing your brand on a friend or an influencer's page.

- Moving down the funnel, **consideration** translates to when your potential consumer looks at your profile page, follows you, or goes to your website.

- The **conversion** phase occurs when the customer ultimately clicks and purchases.

- The **loyalty** step is all about what happens after the first purchase. Does this customer still follow your brand? Does this customer like and comment on all or some of your posts? If so, this person may be more likely to become a repeat customer, allowing your effective and convenient marketing and transaction process to serve as a valuable tool for lowering your customer acquisition costs. A true win-win!

- When discussing the funnel's role within social media, marketers love to point out that social media makes the **advocacy** step extremely easy for satisfied customers. Social media provides a platform for loyal customers to share their love for your brand with their networks and drive people who have never heard of your brand to the top of the funnel with an added bonus: a friend's (or a "friend's") seal of approval, which will ultimately make them more likely to click "buy." This step is one of the most important steps, and it is ultimately why so many brands invest in catchy, eye-popping packaging with the hope that someone out there makes an unboxing video to share.

The Marketing Funnel is so significant in understanding the Instagram economy, because Instagram was the only platform on which you could hit all five steps of the Marketing Funnel in the same place. While you could argue that Facebook is similarly designed to optimize funnel conversion, Instagram was really where the idea that any user could influence their friends, family, and network flourished. (Think about it: do you ever talk about Facebook influencers? No. You talk about Instagram influencers!)

The idea of influence is inherently integral to the loyalty and advocacy steps of the funnel.

WHY THE FUNNEL WORKS BETTER IN THEORY THAN IN PRACTICE

In theory, once you build a network of loyal followers on your business account, you don't have to spend a dime on advertising to convert eyeballs at the top of the funnel into paying customers at the bottom. Of course, this is a best-case (and very unrealistic) scenario, only experienced by the few businesses on Instagram during its Golden Age. To reiterate for those in the back, the Marketing Funnel is simply a theory.

However, with an understanding of how the theoretical Marketing Funnel works, you can see why so many people initially turned to and continue to cite Instagram as the cheapest way to generate sales, because in theory, acquiring customers and making sales can cost zero dollars.

Once brands and marketing teams realized this was even remotely possible, everyone hopped on the bandwagon. Brands were willing to do whatever it took and pay whatever it cost to maximize the amount of people going through each step of their metaphorical funnel. Brands poured money into campaigns that flooded each step of the funnel that, over time, drove demand and subsequent costs for customer acquisition up.

Supply and demand tipped the platform out of favor for businesses. The winner on Instagram was no longer the entrepreneur with the robust ad strategy, but rather Instagram and Facebook as they collected money from your ads. As a result, in practice, the Instagram world as we know it today, along with each step of the funnel, is too crowded and does not allow your brand to flow through each step the way it might have during Instagram's Golden Age.

If your takeaway is that the Marketing Funnel, while still applicable in theory, does not yield the same results in practice anymore, then cue the confetti–you get it!

CHAPTER 7

INSTAGRAM ADS

DIRTY LEMON

If you've heard of the company Dirty Lemon, you have most likely come across an Instagram post featuring a bikini-clad model or celebrity out by the pool of a sponsored Hamptons house, sipping from a striking black-and-white striped glass bottle a few summers ago with a tag directing you to Dirty Lemon's Instagram page.

After seeing the same repetitive visual on Instagram over and over again, it was logical to assume that perhaps new company Dirty Lemon had something to do with beating the heat or maybe even partial nudity. But no, not exactly. Dirty Lemon is a beverage brand, selling wellness drinks for over ten dollars a pop.

In 2015, Dirty Lemon launched on Instagram with a flurry of ads and sponsored posts. As far as the avocado toast generation was concerned, the brand was everywhere. Dirty Lemon's presence was so prolific, it became Instagram-famous itself.

By all accounts, Dirty Lemon was a true Instagram success story. However, sustaining the digital ad spend that had made Dirty Lemon so popular in the first place was becoming impossible. Founder Zak Normandin explains that "the cost for Dirty Lemon to acquire a customer on [the Instagram] platform rose from around $30 in 2017 to more than $100 at the end of 2018."[9]

Spending thirty dollars to acquire a new customer who is ideally purchasing at least one six-pack of your product for sixty-five dollars makes good business sense. But spending $100 to earn sixty-five dollars per customer? That's just bad business. It doesn't take much to recognize that the only way for this model to work is for each acquired customer to become a repeat customer with the catch being that Dirty Lemon is not allowed to spend any more money luring them to return.

In 2019, Dirty Lemon took a new approach to customer acquisition. Zak puts it bluntly: "After spending over $3 million on Instagram and Facebook ads the past year, we're completely shutting off social advertising and transitioning this budget [offline]."[10] Let that sink in.

---

9 Hodgson, Camilla. "How start-ups have used Instagram to build $1bn businesses." Ft.com. https://www.ft.com/content/a5e69d68-4c36-11e9-bbc9-6917dce3dc62. (Accessed January 26, 2020).

10 Stanley, T.L. "Q&A: Dirty Lemon's Founder and Iris Nova CEO on the Future of The Drug Store." Adweek.com. https://www.adweek.com/brand-marketing/qa-dirty-lemons-founder-and-ceo-on-the-future-of-the-drug-store/. (Accessed January 26, 2020).

Dirty Lemon is touted as one of the few brands that mastered the art of the Instagram ad in the first place. For a company that was previously Instagram-exclusive, this seismic shift in advertising dollars is more than significant–it shows how companies can no longer depend on a singular Instagram advertising strategy.

Zak's advice to new brands is crystal clear: "If we were starting from zero right now, we wouldn't start on Facebook or Instagram."[11]

BROOKLINEN

Another direct-to-consumer company famous for its robust Instagram ads is bedding brand Brooklinen, which is known for its crisp millennial-approved aesthetic and, of course, its sheets. When it comes to reaching its core consumer, Brooklinen is one of those brands that nailed it on social media.

In the beginning, Brooklinen was "spending 75 percent of its overall ad budget on Facebook" with impressive results that kept it returning to the platform.[12] However, like so many brands have found out the hard way, this strategy was unsustainable. Brooklinen founder Rich Fulop describes

---

11 Hodgson, Camilla. "How start-ups have used Instagram to build $1bn businesses." Ft.com. https://www.ft.com/content/a5e69d68-4c36-11e9-bbc9-6917dce3dc62. (Accessed January 26, 2020).

12 Liffreing, Ilyse. "Pivot to traditional: Direct-to-consumer brands sour on Facebook ads." Digiday.com. https://digiday.com/marketing/pivot-traditional-direct-consumer-brands-sour-facebook-ads/. (Accessed January 26, 2020).

how the company's cost per impression has doubled year after year. He adds, "we're trying to move away from Facebook as fast as we can ... We're fighting in this little slip of real estate with everyone else out there, and it's hard to cut through. You're paying an impression-based auction, so you are essentially bidding against anybody and everybody that wants to compete for that space, so it's become a hyper-competitive environment."[13] For any brand, increased competition translates to increased expenditure.

Both Dirty Lemon and Brooklinen are bonafide Instagram success stories, and they're abandoning the platform faster than you can say "Hey, check out my new startup!" So why do people keep going back to the well, hoping to recreate a digital advertising strategy that Dirty Lemon and Brooklinen have since abandoned?

THE INITIAL ALLURE OF ADVERTISING ON INSTAGRAM

If you think this chapter is about how to run an effective Instagram advertising campaign, you've come to the wrong place! And if you think that chapter is coming soon...you've come to the wrong book. Instead, I want to outline the why behind how the boom of social media advertising came to be.

---

13 Liffreing, Ilyse. "Pivot to traditional: Direct-to-consumer brands sour on Facebook ads." Digiday.com. https://digiday.com/marketing/pivot-traditional-direct-consumer-brands-sour-facebook-ads/. (Accessed January 26, 2020).

If the top of the Marketing Funnel represents the largest group of people who will see and may organically make their way down the funnel to spend money on your product, the ability to expand that pool at the top will also expand the pool at the bottom. Advertising on Instagram allows you to increase the amount of people in the top "awareness" step of the Marketing Funnel, thus improving your chances of more people shopping your product. This is why brands advertise on social media in the first place.

Additionally, Facebook provides unparalleled access, data, and analytical resources to its advertisers. This is a massive advantage compared to the shot-in-the-dark metrics advertisers of the past relied on while estimating their viewership data after, say, erecting a billboard over a congested highway. Access to precise viewer and shopping data product is an attractive deal that is arguably worth the headache of navigating Facebook's advertising portal.

The ability to increase your total addressable market, the largest possible group of people in the "awareness" step of the marketing funnel–combined with the fact that you now have access to vital information on who these people are, where they are, and how they behave when they see your ad–is why business owners are so eager to advertise on Instagram in the first place.

If only Instagram advertising, like the Marketing Funnel, worked in practice the way it does in theory!

ADVERTISING MADE SIMPLE ... KIND OF

Putting your first ad on social media seems easy enough in the beginning, but if you are doing it right, it's far from easy.

Facebook makes it essentially idiot-proof to start digging yourself into the advertising hole by offering the option to promote almost every single post you put up. It's an attractive deal with rates starting at just one dollar per day. One dollar! Maybe you're feeling risky and want to up that to twenty dollars for your first ad, just to see what happens, or even $100. It doesn't matter, though, because chances are, no matter what number you choose to spend, the results will likely disappoint you right out of the gate.

Why? Because as the Facebook reps will tell you, it takes time for the algorithm to optimize your ads. What that really means is that it takes time, and of course, more money.

Even though Instagram makes it relatively simple to submit an ad for review, (just four clicks away on your phone!) that doesn't mean advertising on the platform is the right move for your business, either.

To get the most out of an advertising campaign on social media, you need to have an expert-level understanding of how the Facebook advertising portal works and not rely on the attractive, in-your-face "promote" button located at the bottom of every single post. This may seem obvious to companies like Dirty Lemon and Brooklinen who have mastered the art of the digital ad. Even bringing up this point in the first place may be laughable because of course you would never click a few buttons and expect instant results. But isn't the fact that this is an option make you a little wary of using Facebook as an advertising tool? I digress ...

HIDDEN COSTS

To make the most of an advertising campaign, you need to have multiple (sometimes hundreds of) variations of your creative content and to continually tweak your ad sets weekly, and sometimes daily. This gets expensive.

Be warned: for some companies, the expense of hiring an expert, team, or agency to manage the ads on top of the ad spend is worth it. But for others, when your advertising cost to acquire a new customer is equal to your average order value, you are still in the hole for the added expenses spent on running the campaign itself.

Not surprisingly, the business of being frustrated by Instagram ads is also booming!

Digital marketing agencies, consultants, specialists, courses, and the like have seemingly popped up out of nowhere to help struggling entrepreneurs create social ads that actually work (for real this time). Of course, for their services, it's going to cost you money on top of what you're spending on the actual ads.

Right off the bat, many of these companies will tell you that your first mistake was not calling them sooner, but rest assured, they can map out a dynamic campaign with tens to hundreds of ad variations targeting different subgroups within your target demographic. Success with social media ads requires a ton of testing, time, and work up front, not the simple click-and-buy option you have available to you on your phone. But what these digital marketing specialists don't tell you is that your second mistake is relying on ads alone in the first place.

Once again, the myth that Instagram ads and Instagram ads alone will get you to reach your sales goals is perpetuated, and it's all because of our unwillingness to let go of our perceived version of the past and accept that Instagram's Glory Days are over.

EXPECTATIONS VERSUS REALITY

In 2017, Rooshy Roy founded her skincare line, Aavrani, intending to drive sales with an Instagram-first marketing strategy.

Rooshy was an MBA candidate at Wharton when she decided to take the entrepreneurial leap. At Wharton, the birthplace of Warby Parker and subsequent "*Warby Parkers of*," joining in on the direct-to-consumer fun that her peers and notable alumni were having was a no-brainer.

Rooshy knew about the void in the market for traditional Indian skincare, the kind she had been making in her kitchen with her mom growing up. So, she developed a product oozing with tried-and-true rituals her ancestors spent centuries perfecting–chock-full of native Indian ingredients like turmeric, neem oil, and honey–and then she brought it mainstream.

During her initial market research, Rooshy noticed a common thread among direct-to-consumer beauty brands: the pervasive reliance on an Instagram-first marketing strategy. This can be explained by the fact that these brands were selling direct-to-consumer products in the beauty space where Glossier and its best practices, from packaging to customer acquisition, were seen as the industry standard.

The year 2017 was also when the direct-to-consumer landscape was inundated with new brands each and every day, all coming onto the scene in hopes of the same online success Warby Parker enjoyed. All you had to do was replicate Warby's model, right? In an environment like Wharton–now known as part business school and part startup incubator thanks to Warby Parker's formative years on campus–starting out digitally with a heavy focus on a paid ad strategy seemed the only way forward. If it ain't broke, don't fix it ... right?

However, when it came time to launch Aavrani's digital ad strategy, Rooshy was surprised and disappointed by her dismal returns from her Instagram ads. She elaborates, "The conversions on Instagram were absolutely lower than what I expected, because the brands that have really been able to leverage Instagram, like Glossier and other digitally native brands in that 2014-2015 era, capped out on that opportunity.

I learned that you cannot replicate that strategy anymore. It took that trial and error [period] to realize that even a few years later, you can't just replicate what Warby Parker and Glossier did on social media and expect it to work today."

Rooshy is one of many founders who realized after going all in on an Instagram-first marketing strategy that it's not all it's cracked up to be. But when Rooshy began meeting with investors to take her business to the next level, another unforeseen, yet related problem cropped up. "I didn't really learn this until I went out in the market and started fundraising when investors kept asking, 'What's your customer acquisition strategy?' And I started to notice that investors, especially the more astute or up-to-speed they were with the beauty industry, would get wary of strategies around paid ads, because even they know from their own portfolios that it's not a long-term strategy. And maybe it's not even a near-term strategy anymore."

Learning that investors were no longer sold on the glorified paid advertising strategy of Instagram's Golden Age came as a shock to Rooshy, especially considering some of the most heavily funded brands today are still seen using paid ads and receiving the money to fund these ads directly from investors. However, the key difference is that as a new company today, Rooshy's customer acquisition costs would be significantly higher from the get-go because of the modern advertising landscape we find ourselves in.

Rooshy reflected on the skeptical responses she received from potential investors. Combined with the low returns from her advertising strategy, she knew she had to recalibrate fast. Fortunately, Rooshy quickly revamped her strategy, deemphasizing paid ads and focusing more on traditional PR and community building. Entrepreneurs and investors alike are learning that when starting a company from scratch, a robust Insta-advertising strategy will not work the way it used to. Accepting this is the first step, while recalibrating your marketing plan accordingly is the second–albeit more difficult–step.

GO HOME! THE PARTY'S OVER

We now know that back in the Golden Age, Instagram ads were relatively inexpensive compared to preexisting advertising options, and they were underpriced compared to what they're going for now.

While it wasn't free, a large-scale online campaign was nowhere near as costly as a television campaign or a traditional media buy in a magazine. If your ads weren't working online, you could also pull them immediately instead of bleeding money that you knew wouldn't yield your desired results while your ad termed. Plus, with social media advertising, you had analytics at your fingertips and the ability to test different images, copy, and other variables you felt could impact the ad with just a few clicks.

For businesses used to throwing ad dollars down a black hole and hoping for a positive return with customers making their way down the Marketing Funnel, Instagram's analytics and insights became a very attractive selling point.

But today's market has changed with the cost of Facebook and Instagram ads skyrocketing far beyond the affordable option they used to be. This increased cost, coupled with the additional expenses it requires to create and run a successful advertising campaign, does not make for smart business anymore.

Gary Vaynerchuk–founder of the highly-respected digital marketing agency VaynerMedia, serial entrepreneur, and now a full-blown Insta-celebrity himself, known as the DJ Khaled of side hustlers–was eager to tout the effectiveness and efficiency of social media advertisements, specifically Google ads, at the 2017 SXSW Conference.[14]

Gary foreshadowed our current digital marketing environment, comparing the basement-level prices of Google ads in the early aughts (2001-2003) to the prices of Facebook and Instagram ads in 2017. He told the crowd all about taking his family's wine business digital when online advertising was this new, novel tool. He elaborates, "When I stand up here and say I built my dad's [wine] store from three to sixty million dollars, I always feel that it should have been $250 million, because what I didn't do was spend all my money on Google Adwords in 2001, '02, and '03."

Gary deems these unbelievably low rates as "historically amazing," and we all know the cost to advertise on Google

14 Clifford, Catherine. "Social media guru: Facebook video is the best ad buy for your money right now." CNBC.com. https://www.cnbc.com/2017/03/17/social-media-guru-facebook-video-is-the-best-value-ad-buy-right-now.html. (Accessed January 26, 2020).

today will most likely never be as affordable as it was during its nascent years. Gary regrets not taking more advantage of the advertising options Google was offering during the early days and warned business owners not to fall victim to the identical scenario that is playing out with Facebook and Instagram ads today.

He continued to draw parallels between the early days of Google and Facebook with regard to ad pricing options, noting that in 2017, "We [were] paying six to thirteen dollar CPM [cost per thousand impressions] on Facebook right now that are going to be fifty to eighty dollars in thirty-six and forty-eight months, and everybody is going to be sad that they didn't jump on it,"

He makes a great point, but it's important to remember that this was in 2017. So, don't dive in just yet!

It's safe to say that in 2020, we've officially reached the days when Facebook and Instagram ads are no longer the inexpensive option they once were. Take it from Gary: if you didn't cash in on social media's basement-level ad pricing at its lowest valuation, it's now best to look elsewhere in your quest to convert eyeballs into dollar signs.

CHAPTER 8

HIDDEN COSTS

KITTY AND VIBE

Cameron Armstrong had a crotch problem, and she knew she couldn't possibly be the only woman who experienced this.

She was sick and tired of the way bathing suits are designed to fit you in the waist, but not in the crotch. She found that with a few simple tweaks to the "kitty" area, swimsuits would fit better, and the women who routinely experience too much or too little fabric in the back no longer have that problem with her new sizing metric.

As a Gen-Z entrepreneur who started her business in 2018, Cameron knew right off the bat that Instagram would be important to her company's success and community building. Capitalizing on her crotch-first focus, she injected a force of female humor and energy into her brand and corresponding Instagram programming.

For her Instagram content strategy, Cameron allocates a budget toward producing a mix of professional product images and model photography to show off her products. But from an Instagram metrics standpoint, these images, which are expensive to produce, do not necessarily guarantee returns in the form of likes and comments like her other posts do.

In addition to boasting professional imagery, Kitty and Vibe's Instagram account is full of free user-generated content, quotes, and memes. Cameron notes, "It's really frustrating when I have this beautiful photo from one of our shoots that's so representative of the brand, is so diverse, it's really high quality and just a gorgeous photo that will flop [from a likes and engagement perspective], and then a meme of Jonathan Van Ness will skyrocket."

On a platform oversaturated with brands trying to sell, sell, sell, this makes sense. Regardless of whether you're putting money behind professionally shot product posts for the Instagram scroller, staged shots are effectively an advertisement. And on Instagram, ads are not what people want. The consumer is still looking to be entertained and scroll for fun, and when a "fun" post pops up on their feed, they are more likely to toss it a like. And the more likes a post gets, the higher it ranks in the algorithm, exposing it to more people who can like it, too.

Cameron continues,"For a business account, a mix [of content] is really important because at this point, customers are so smart and know that the channel has become such a marketplace. And sometimes they just want to use Instagram, not spend any money, and see culturally relevant and funny, uplifting, and engaging content that isn't forcing you to buy something."

It's a balance for brands to find ways to connect with prospective shoppers on an emotional level while ultimately trying to get them to shop from you once they buy into the brand. However, the frustrating reality is that the content you spend the most money on creating for social is not necessarily the content that is going to get you the most engagement, likes, and ultimately sales.

WHY BOTHER?

So why do entrepreneurs bother paying so much to produce content for their brand's Instagram page? Despite their high cost, these professional shots are essential to a brand's image roster.

For Kitty and Vibe, photoshoots are the best way to showcase its unique approach to the crotch problem their competitors have ignored for generations. Professional photography and videos allow companies to "show instead of tell" their story in a way that differentiates them from other swimsuit brands.

Product photography is a necessary expense, especially as brands use their Instagram feeds as a digital catalogue of their offerings, so they treat their product posts as such. Increasingly, shoppers are going to Instagram *first* to check out the new brand they just heard of to see what they're all about, so first impressions count more than ever.

Knowing this, a company wouldn't send out a catalogue full of blurry pictures of wrinkled wares to prospective customers, would it? No way! Your catalogue would feature the best of the best photography only, shot with great lighting and a steamer on set (though not visible in the frame, of course).

At this point, consumers are conditioned to a certain level of Insta-product photography standards that brands must have in order to compete. When the competition is high, your quality has to be higher.

Brands have to reconcile the fact that their made-for-Instagram content is going to cost them big bucks, and the metrics that Instagram has conditioned us to use in determining whether or not a post is "good" or "bad" no longer apply in considering the success of your product-only photography, because the goals are different now. Instead of shooting for likes, the money spent on expensive imagery is more about branding, creating an online catalogue, and defining your "vibe."

...BUT IT'S FREE?!

We know now that just because it's free to download and set up, a business account on Instagram is anything but free. When it comes to using Instagram for business today, you get what you pay for.

Gone are the days when posting iPhone photos would lead to a steady stream of sales on your website. Increasingly, brands are investing in everything from content to strategy to implementation and community management...just to get started. From a budget perspective, these costs add up.

Brands are still able to take advantage of Instagram's free offerings to leverage their feeds, like reposting user-generated content and quickly adapting their strategy to capitalize on any new Instagram feature (which, when done right and early enough, rumor has it that Instagram's algorithm will be more likely to expand the reach on that particular post.) But entrepreneurs and experts alike report that a healthy mix of costly staged imagery with everything else is still the best way to go.

CONTENT CREATION AND BEYOND

Instagram was founded to be a photo-sharing app, a place to post pictures of you and your friends and family doing whatever it is that you do. It was intended as a highlight reel of your life's greatest moments. And now, as we know, the app meant for sharing wedding photos is now used for marketing initiatives to sell things like bowties.

Comparing the success rate of a wedding photo to an image of a bowtie is comparing freshly picked apples to moldy, rotten oranges. Even without the help (or "help," depending on how you look at it) of the Instagram algorithm–designed to broadcast your wedding photos to more people than it will show your bowtie picture to–people are going to inherently care more about your wedding than your bowtie, no matter what.

And so begins the rat race of attempting to create content for bowties and other consumer goods that will perform *close* to that of a wedding picture on Instagram.

As far as creating content goes, entrepreneurs are familiar with routinely shelling out cash every time they launch a new product. Sure, you can bootstrap your content to a degree, and hopefully you have a friend who is fluent in Photoshop, Lightroom, and video creation, but with the sheer volume of brands all vying for the same eyeballs, entrepreneurs need to heavily invest in their content to stand a chance.

When competition increases, so do the costs of produce competitive imagery. A high-resolution image of your product against an ambiguous background used to be sufficient when it came to a product photo, but given the increasingly competitive landscape, this framework would now appear old, dated, and even worse ... cheap!

Now, to help break through the noise of Instagram, photography cost considerations include everything from lighting and trendy backdrops to national park permits. Because really, if you haven't shot your product from all angles, surrounded by the Insta-famous Antelope Canyon in Arizona, did you really expect to stand out from your competition?

Christina Brillati, the owner of photography studio Tribe Detroit, founded a program aptly named Snap + Social + Solve to help entrepreneurs cut down on hidden photography costs. The program aims to be a one-stop-shop, "an efficient and effective solution for one of the biggest problems facing small businesses today–creating content for your business." You bring your product, and Snap + Social + Solve provides everything else.[15]

Christina notes that for $600, brands can leave her studio with over 100 Insta-ready images. Combine these photos at six dollars a pop with user-generated content, relevant quotes, and whatever else you deem on brand, and you've just stockpiled half a year's worth of content at a great price.

In addition to saving yourself the opportunity cost and stress of setting up your own photoshoot, you've likely saved your business tens of thousands of dollars. (That's not even factoring in the flight to Antelope Canyon!)

RECONCILING THE SPEND

Entrepreneurs were particularly tight-lipped when I asked how much they spent per post on Instagram. Many were quick to acknowledge that the amount was more than they'd like to be spending, but even still, they felt ever-increasing pressure to allocate larger portions of their budgets toward creating the perfect Instagram image.

---

15 Tribe Detroit. "Snap + Social + Solve." Tribedetroit.com. https://tribedetroit.com/snap-social-solve/. (accessed January 26, 2020).

Knowing how much these expensive images cost combined with the fact that they are not going to be their top performers on social, entrepreneurs are looking to repurpose this expensive imagery in other marketing initiatives, which certainly helps to soften the blow.

Photographer Alisha Siegel finds that "product photography costs have definitely gone up, everything from booking more expensive shoot locations to getting custom-made props. All aspects about the process are getting more sophisticated, and it is directly because of Instagram's impact on what it takes to showcase your product. Having said that, I am now noticing my clients who were previously booking Instagram-exclusive content shoots want pictures that they can use more broadly, like for marketing initiatives and even mailers and postcards."

Repurposing your made-for-Instagram photography is a great way to make the most of your previously social media-exclusive content. With offline marketing initiatives growing in popularity, it is clear that traditional marketing tactics will be *en vogue* once again. With this in mind, be sure to leave every photoshoot with usable images in all shapes, sizes, and aspect ratios.

CHAPTER 9

EVERYTHING LOOKS THE SAME

IS IT ME, OR...?

If you feel like all the brands you see on Instagram in the direct-to-consumer space look the same, no, you're not going crazy! It's because they do. From the products to the branding styles to the way they market, brands aren't just blending together–they are carbon copies with a different logo splashed on the box.

As mentioned, it's never been easier to start a company, specifically one in the consumer goods space. Whether you're inventing a new product from scratch or putting a fresh spin on an existing model, all you need is an internet connection to get started.

You don't even need an idea! Companies like Oberlo are in the business of selling templated e-commerce ideas with fully integrated drop shipping infrastructure that can be executed with just the click of a button. Or, if that isn't your thing, you can see what everyone else is doing (bed linens, anyone? How about some comfortable bras in a variety of skin tones? Anyone need another sock subscription?) and put your signature touch on it, hoping that is enough to make you stand out in the crowd.

With every brand trying to stand out, do any actually succeed in doing so?

THE SAME PRODUCTS

When so many new direct-to-consumer products across categories are begging for your attention, how do you know which ones to support? And, even trickier: how do you differentiate one company that sells trendy cookware from the other two that are targeting you at the same time?

If you have shopped for a mattress (or Googled one once) in the last year or so, you have no doubt been inundated with ads from various mattress companies all trying to persuade you to pick them over the competition. The added bonus is that you don't even have to go into a store to buy them. These new mattresses are delivered straight to your door, usually in a box that is easy to carry and unpack in just a few minutes.

The old-school way of buying a mattress was not the most pleasant experience, but it got the job done. You would go to your local mattress store, speak with an associate, and explain your needs and desired firmness. Eventually, you would be pointed in the direction of a few mattresses at varying price points and get to hop (or flop) on each one, testing them all out before buying one. Since you don't buy mattresses very often (let's say you are purchasing a new one every ten years), the experience isn't too terrible.

However, nothing is immune to disruption these days, especially by entrepreneurs in the direct-to-consumer space. And so it was decided that the mattress store experience was in need of an upgrade. New entrants to the mattress industry promised big, exciting things: We'll deliver a mattress straight to your door, and you don't have to even set foot inside a tired mattress store ever again. With a healthy injection of funding, new direct-to-consumer mattress brands like Casper, Leesa, Nectar, Purple, and Tuft & Needle burst onto the scene around the same time and in full force.

Today, an estimated 175+ direct-to-consumer bed-in-a-box companies all offer the same value proposition: no more shopping at a mattress store ever again.[16] In looking under the hood, it's clear that not just their mission statements are the same–the products themselves are also eerily similar.

In response to the influx of new delivered-to-your-doorstep mattress companies, the founder of GoodBed.com Michael

16 Wu, Jasmine. "There are now 175 online mattress companies—and you can't tell them apart." CNBC.com. https://www.cnbc.com/2019/08/18/there-are-now-175-online-mattress-companiesand-you-cant-tell-them-apart.html. (accessed January 26, 2020).

Magnuson tells CNBC that "none of these guys, with a few rare exceptions, make their own mattresses." He claims that they all use the same four main mattress manufacturers that have been around forever, meaning their products are nearly identical as well. Sounds a lot like the Luxottica situation, right? Yikes.

Since the majority of these mattress brands blend together and their product offerings are quite similar, what's the difference between the mattresses of today and the mattresses of the past? No dingy mattress stores. Some new, flashy marketing. And some minor upgrades in technology. But that's it.

The problem on the brand side is that since these new players have removed the store from the equation, they're looking to market online, as is the nature of the digitally native direct-to-consumer model. But of course, with over 175 new mattress companies all vying for the same digital ad space on your Instagram feeds, their costs to advertise on social media are skyrocketing because when everything looks the same and is the same, the only way to beat out the competition is to be the company spending the most.

In industries with low barriers to entry like the mattress industry (bed linens, underwear, socks), competition is growing fiercer by the day. With more competition online that all appears identical, costs to advertise on Instagram go up, which renders Instagram an inefficient use of capital when trying to reach new customers.

THE SAME BRANDS

For decades, consumers have known or at the very least had a hunch that the cosmetics sold in drugstores are very similar (if not identical) to the high-end options in department stores, because they are all produced at the same factories. When we opt for the Yves Saint Laurent lipstick at a department store over the L'Oréal lipstick at the drugstore (both made in the same factory in nearly identical colors), for example, we are buying into the YSL brand more than anything else. We are opting for a more luxurious lip staining experience by way of the brand's perceived value and pay a price for it.

Since we know a lot of these products are essentially the same once removed from their pretty packaging, we look to branding to distinguish one from the other. The problem here is that lately, a lot of the branding is also looking the same.

The minimalist fonts. All the extra white space. Clean lines. To-the-point messaging. Generic. Simple. Risk-averse. You can probably think of ten new-ish brands that fit this mold right off the top of your head. Big, well-funded names started to follow an unspoken Instagram-friendly brand template, and now lesser-known startup brands are following along because it appears to "work." But does it actually? If we're noticing it now, we're most likely becoming immune to the effects of minimalist design used to sell us an upgraded version of a product we already have. Think: mattresses, razors, contact lenses, and more.

The name for this trend? "Blanding." Coined by Thierry Brunfaut and Tom Greenwood, blanding is a branding strategy that strips down a brand down to just a few letters and colors. And it's everywhere.[17]

"The formula is sort of a brand paint-by-numbers. Start with a made-up-word name. Put it in a sans-serif typeface. Make it clean and readable, with just the right amount of white space. Use a direct tone of voice. Nope, no need for a logo. Maybe throw in some cheerful illustrations. Just don't forget the vibrant colors. Bonus points for purple and turquoise. Blah blah blah. And I do mean blah."

Perhaps this strategy worked for a time, but that time is over.

In an article for *Fast Company,* design writer Mark Wilson explores this shift and speaks with a branding insider about this very point. "I think history has proven itself over and over again that when sameness hits a saturation point, it plateaus. I also think it's kind of shortsighted on the design profession's part to underestimate millennials–that their taste level is so inherently limited that they'd be satisfied forever with a reductive palette and a single formula. We've seen young people rebel against the status quo, and I think they'll react to the sameness in the brand landscape. It's a matter of time."[18]

---

17 Brunfaut, Thierry. Greenwood, Tom. "The hottest branding trend of the year is also the worst." Fastcompany.com. https://www.fastcompany.com/90276496/the-hottest-branding-trend-of-the-year-is-also-the-worst. (accessed January 26, 2020).

18 Wilson, Mark. "Why so many brands on Instagram look the same." Fastcompany.com. https://www.fastcompany.com/90281112/why-so-many-brands-on-instagram-look-the-same. (accessed January 26, 2020).

When it comes to branding, businesses must recognize that the consumer is over the watered-down version of whatever it is they're selling. Because it seems like everyone else is doing it, utilizing this branding strategy is counterintuitive to the entire ethos of what it means to build a good brand.

If you're looking to stand out in your industry, you have to be unique. As the old adage goes, just because everyone else is doing it, does not mean you should do it, too.

THE SAME MARKETING MATERIALS

In today's business landscape, the endless supply of marketing materials required to effectively run an e-commerce, social-facing business requires a lot of time, effort, and money. In order to keep up with rigorous Instagram posting schedules, brands are constantly increasing their budgets while chalking it up to a justifiable marketing spend.

The problem is that as brands spend more and more money developing content, they want to ensure this content is going to generate sufficient likes and comments, which can be seen (and judged) at the bottom of each post. While brands attempt to churn out posts guaranteed to perform well, the posts all start to blend together and look the same.

In an article about Instagram for *Business of Fashion,* writer Amy Odell speaks to this issue, saying that "millions of Instagram user–influencers, included–feel pressured to post content that's sure to perform over and over again, resulting in sameness in their feeds and on the platform as a whole. Wouldn't it be nice if Instagram moved on from cappuccinos and farmer's market fruit? It's similar to the problem that plagues digital publishers: too much attention to data leads to content created for the purpose of hitting numbers rather than pleasing actual people."[19] Instead of branching out and attempting to be unique, brands are increasingly relying on the same style of content across the board. And it shows.

Photographer Alisha Siegel started her career in e-commerce working for Fab.com, a website known for its hard-to-find quirky products and kitschy offerings. She developed an eye for photography and left to start her own photography firm in 2014. Alisha's business benefited tremendously from the onslaught of entrepreneurs needing a seemingly endless supply of digital images. Alisha found her schedule fully booked months in advance with shoots requested for the sole purpose of creating content suitable for social media. However, it seemed that no matter how varied their product offerings might be, from scarves to fitness equipment, her clients all wanted to shoot their products in the exact same way.

Alisha explains, "I used to go on Instagram and Pinterest to find different photography styles and techniques, but it's becoming harder and harder to find things that are unique because everything is blending together at the moment.

---

19 Odell, Amy. "Hiding 'Likes' Is Good for the Influencer Economy." Businessoffashion.com. https://www.businessoffashion.com/articles/professional/how-hiding-likes-is-good-for-the-influencer-economy. (accessed January 26, 2020).

Certain styles really work on Instagram, like the super high flash photography with products arranged in a way that look like they are being set up like a traditional still life painting, a style that Glossier really pioneered. And then everyone was copying them and doing that for years. And I get it because Glossier has a large following and for them, it seems to work. So, my clients, the entrepreneurs or their creative teams, all want their products to be shot the same way as Glossier. It's as if someone decided 'there's only one way to shoot a tube of lipstick' and it's the only way. So, if you're wondering why everything looks the same, it's because it is!"

While Alisha has been able to leverage the constant need for product imagery in our Insta-focused world to build up a client list, she expresses frustration at the overall dependence on and adherence to trends. "I, like so many photographers right now, have had to pivot and cater towards this audience that expects to see products shot in a certain way and it's infuriating because I know there are so many better, more unique ways to shoot a product!"

Cookie cutter content is a short-term fix.

Sure, as an entrepreneur looking at the initial data from your social media content, your brand will most likely see a strong showing of likes and comments from that now-ironic overhead avocado toast shot, but over time, a dependence on these cheap wins will drown you out. Instead, the brands who take risks will be the only ones getting noticed.

At the same time, an entire photo studio industry is growing out of brands' needs for similar looking professional content. With an emphasis on photography that appears organic yet aspirational, homes that are fully furnished and have been curated for the sole purpose of shooting Instagram photos are cropping up all over the country.

The Village Studio is one such company curating these Insta-ready rooms. Designed as a loft in Soho, the space boasts a variety of Insta-perfect moments, like a millennial pink velvet couch scene, a spotless kitchen with gold accents, a serene bathtub moment, a productive, yet clutter free office setting, and more. With such high demand for their space, Village Studio is opening two new locations this year–one in Brooklyn and one in Los Angeles.

THE SAME CUTTING BOARDS

People are starting to take note of this over-curated content.

A recent Instagram post from Jessica Alba features her standing in a gorgeous, white kitchen with a dreamy island in front of her and perfectly arranged oversized wooden cutting boards behind her. Jessica's hair is done, and she is posing comfortably for the camera with an array of kids' products strewn about. In the post, she boasts the benefits of making healthy choices for her children, specifically addressing the pros of Culturelle Probiotics, the sponsor of this post.

In a separate, yet also sponsored Instagram post, Kate Hudson is seen in the same exact kitchen, with the white walls, dreamy island and perfectly arranged oversized wooden cutting boards behind her, preaching the benefits of using Weight Watchers on her postpartum journey.

Two different celebrities. Two different brands. The same exact kitchen.[20]

Fans were quick to point out that had it not been for the ridiculously oversized cutting boards, this rented kitchen snafu could have gone unnoticed by the general public. Instead, the cutting boards that represented relatability and a family-centric lifestyle were the dead giveaway. While not the most embarrassing Insta-error a celebrity can make these days by a long shot, the incident offered a peek into the sameness we are experiencing in increasing amounts on our Instagram feeds.

SO IT'S NOT JUST ME? GOOD!

Nope, it's not just you. From the products themselves, to the repetitive brand styles, to the identical marketing techniques, everything on Instagram is starting to look the same. And potential shoppers are starting to catch on to the formulaic nature of building a brand on Instagram, leading to frustration, confusion, and overall fatigue.

---

20 Hafer, Dylan. "You'll die when you see Jessica Alba's latest #spon fail." Betches.com. https://betches.com/youll-die-when-you-see-jessica-albas-latest-spon-fail/. (accessed January 26, 2020).

On the consumer side, when everything appears to be homogeneous, how do you know which product to shop? How do you figure out which witty copy resonates the most and will ultimately convince you to click "buy"? How do you weigh the choice between one company that features a promotional deal with a multicultural family using the company's products and its competitor also featuring a promotional deal with a multicultural family using its products?

As an entrepreneur, scrolling through the feeds of the most popular Instagram brands might lead you to believe in a designated mold that works, from the products themselves to the marketing materials used. Understandably, you might be tempted to apply this marketing framework to your own business. Yet, this approach to attacking the market is short-sighted. If anything, consider the repetitive nature of what everyone else is doing as a clear-cut template of what not to do when positioning your brand.

CHAPTER 10

THE VALUE OF FOLLOWERS

STONE FOX BRIDE

By all accounts, Founder of Stone Fox Bride Molly Guy had everything an entrepreneur dreams of when founding a company in the Instagram Age: a social media-friendly business that boasted mass appeal, selling the idea of love and supermodel looks to go with it.

Stone Fox Bride was a wedding dress company for cool girls who refused to fit the mold the strait-laced bridal industry was selling. And isn't that something every bride wants for themselves? To be the one bride who is a little bit different, a lot cooler and way more special than all the other brides who came before her? This is the essence of Stone Fox Bride.

Women followed Molly and Stone Fox Bride on social media for her perspective on romance, proposal stories, engagement rings, and wedding dresses. Molly positioned herself as an expert on love who happened to have it all: a handsome husband, a profitable business, and a trendy apartment in Brooklyn. She amassed a large following on social media and was, by all accounts, a successful and enviable entrepreneur of the digital age.

What's more? Following the boom of her business and influential social media presence, Molly signed a book deal for her first hardcover titled *Stone Fox Bride: Love, Lust, and Wedding Planning for the Wild at Heart.*

This achievement would serve as a milestone in the career of any successful entrepreneur, and it provided Molly with another platform on which she could share her thoughts on love and give her expert perspective on planning a cooler-than-fairytale wedding. It would turn out to be the book anybody who's anybody would gift her newly engaged best friend. Best of all, Molly's book would further cement her status as an icon within the wedding industry, as if she hadn't already accomplished this with the spectacular growth of her business and prolific social media presence.

Stone Fox Bride's social media strategy included an aspirational mix of engagement rings, love stories, wedding decor and bridal inspiration. Stemming from her days in the magazine world, each caption was written in Molly's signature writing style with details and emotion oozing from the screen. It was a better-than-Pinterest take on love, and each post was validated by Molly's cool girl tastemaker stamp of approval.

Girls would run up to Molly in her Brooklyn neighborhood and approach her on the subway begging her to take a picture of their engagement rings and to listen to their love stories, with the hope that Molly would maybe, hopefully, one day, post their editorialized love story on her Instagram account. Stone Fox Bride amassed a cult-like following of women, who wanted love, believed in love, and for lack of a better phrase, romanticized love.

But behind the scenes, Molly's life was quickly turning into a different story. Her marriage was falling apart, and her dad was terminally ill. Her public persona, which hinged on highlighting the joys of love, relationships, and weddings, was beginning to feel like a sham.

Business being business, she continued writing and posting about stylized, better-than-Pinterest-perfect weddings and hid her personal life from all but a few close friends for months. Understandably, Molly felt as though she could not announce her impending divorce before the debut of her book on weddings. Not only would her credibility be shot, but she would risk torpedoing the success of the book.

So, she stayed quiet. Eventually, the personal challenges Molly was facing led her to make the difficult decision to shutter her business and to walk away from the wedding industry for good.

After her book was released, her divorce was in motion, and her father had passed away, Molly had finally had enough. In speaking to *The New York Times,* Molly said she was over keeping up the "patina that I had things under control."[21] She opened up to her followers, telling them the reality of her marriage and in-process divorce. She started shying away from posting about love and transitioned her Instagram feed to posting about what was actually happening in her life. The truth.

On Instagram, the fallout was instant. From the moment Molly stopped posting about engagement rings and weddings, she began losing thousands of followers per month, for months on end.[22]

It became clear the majority of Molly's Instagram followers she had amassed over the years had far more interest in her boho-chic wedding content than they did in her father's death, her divorce, her life as a single mother, or the pain she felt shuttering a business she had poured her heart and soul into.

Molly changed the name of her Instagram from Stone Fox Bride to Stone Fox Ride, to signify the new journey she had embarked on and the freedom she felt as she entered a new chapter in her life. While Molly was still the same person behind the account, her followers were still in decline.

---

21 Jones, Allie. "What Happens When a Weddings Influencer Gets Divorced?" NYtimes.com. https://www.nytimes.com/2019/12/10/style/stone-fox-bride-molly-guy-divorce.html. (accessed January 26, 2020).

22 Social Blade. (2020). Stone Fox Ride's Instagram. https://socialblade.com/instagram/user/stonefoxride (accessed February 12, 2020).

Undeterred, Molly continued to post content that was meaningful to her and representative of her current feelings. For many Instagram account owners, posting content you know for a fact is going to lose you followers is one of the biggest no-nos in the game. However, Molly refused to sugarcoat her life for the 'Gram, despite what "good business practices" in the Instagram world would suggest.

The followers who had stayed loyal to Molly and her journey were in for a treat.

The same person they fell in love with who'd preached the power of love was now preaching the power of truth with the same passion and trademark style that had led them to follow her in the first place. Molly's signature writing style was all over her new and improved Instagram presence, despite the fact that nary an engagement ring was in sight.

Notably, Molly grew and blossomed the Stone Fox Ride fanbase into a creative writing community, stemming from Molly's literary expertise, her raw and authentic Instagram captions, and the success of her book.

Today, Molly's writing classes routinely fill up, and if you're wondering where she finds new students, the answer is, of course, through Instagram. By being honest and not focusing on keeping up follower growth for the sake of follower growth, Molly has been able to reach a more actively engaged audience of women with a more genuine and powerful message than she ever could have imagined as Stone Fox Bride.

TAKEAWAYS

Despite the fact that her Instagram follower count was in temporary freefall, a disastrous social media metric by any conventional standard, Molly proved that by staying true to what was most important to her, she could tap into her core audience more effectively. She was able to cut through the noise and reach the people who were most interested in her new business, which happens to be a derivative of her old business.

Had Molly been focused solely on growth like you're "supposed to" in the Insta-world, none of this would have been possible. She might never have told the truth about her broken marriage, which ultimately led to developing her writing course.

For business owners and marketing teams who have poured money into an Instagram growth strategy, are stuck adhering to expert strategies, and never stray from strict supposed "best practices," Molly's story is puzzling. It's the exact opposite of what we're used to hearing about using Instagram as a business tool—that you are supposed to place growing a large following above all else.

VANITY METRICS

The biggest takeaway from Molly's story is when it comes to attracting and retaining followers, the goal should always be to strive for quality over quantity, instead of focusing on vanity metrics. Your follower count is irrelevant if the people who follow you don't actually care about your brand or your content. While vanity metrics may look pretty at the top of your Instagram page, they lack the substance that comes with cultivating a meaningful audience.

CHEAP TRICKS

In a race to build your brand, it can be tempting to employ desperate tactics to grow your numbers and create the appearance that your brand has already attracted swarms of engaged followers.

Common Cheap Trick #1: Many people fall victim to the practice of buying robot followers from sketchy websites to keep up with the Instagram popularity contest. If you want, you can even hop on a plane to Moscow and hit up a vending machine specifically designed to fill your account with likes and comments. For just eighty-nine cents, "you can make sure your selfie gets the extra 100 fake Instagram likes it deserves. For double the price ($1.78) you can purchase 100 Instagram followers."[23] But, come on, you're better than this! Inflating and falsifying your Instagram presence while trying to build a respectable business is an oxymoron and utterly detrimental to your bottom line. Plus, you are positioning yourself in the same way Kim Jong-un does

23 Matsakis, Louise. "This Russian Vending Machine Will Sell You Fake Instagram Likes." Vice.com. https://www.vice.com/en_us/article/xw8yv3/russian-vending-machine-fake-instagram-likes. (accessed January 26, 2020).

when he insists on Photoshopping massive fake crowds behind him at all his "events." It's embarrassing.

Common Cheap Trick #2: With just a little more elbow grease, brands can try to game the system by offering a circuit giveaway or a sweepstakes with other similar-sized accounts. This can provide a short-term solution, as you may see a sudden boost in your follower count and engagement levels, but typically you will lose these new followers as soon as your sweepstakes ends because these new "fans" followed your brand for one reason and one reason only: a chance to win whatever it is you were giving away. Meanwhile, your brand's credibility is taking a direct hit in front of the entire Instagram ecosystem, right where it hurts the most.

Less Common, But Still A Cheap Trick #3: If you remain undeterred and have cash to burn, you can shell out the big bucks to hire a company like Curated Businesses, which promises to mobilize the Kardashian Instagram marketing machine to promote your brand. The Kardashians have hundreds of millions of followers, so it can seem tempting to pay for that type of exposure. Essentially, you are betting on the sheer volume of their network to grow your brand. But let's take a look at why this is a waste of your marketing budget.

The underlying idea behind this strategy is that your brand would pay to become one of the sponsors of an enticing giveaway; think suitcases full of cash and twenty Chanel bags that Kim Kardashian herself is posting about on her personal account. To enter to win, contestants must follow all seventy-five or so brands who are also sponsoring this give-away. By insisting that participants follow every single brand included, Curated Businesses offers these brands exposure to the Kardashian family's entire legion of followers, well into the hundreds of millions of people.

In an exposé titled, "Are Those Obnoxious Kardashian Instagram Giveaways Fake? An Investigation," Dylan Hafer goes in-depth on how Curated Businesses campaigns work, and what's most fascinating is just how much brands are willing to pay to be involved.[24] Dylan finds that brands routinely spend between $25,000 and $50,000 to be included in one of these high-visibility campaigns.

However, when all is said and done, paying a company to attempt to enlist a small fraction of 100 million or so people to follow your brand doesn't necessarily guarantee that these followers are right for your business or that they will remain followers once the contest is over. It certainly doesn't help your sales goals, which is disappointing considering you're now out $25,000-$50,000.

Understand that growing your follower count for the sake of improved optics is a short-term solution that will not result in sustainable increased revenue for your business. It will not help your bottom line in any significant way. Businesses

24 Hafer, Dylan. "Are Those Obnoxious Kardashian Instagram Giveaways Fake? An Investigation." Betches.com. https://betches.com/are-those-obnoxious-kardashian-instagram-giveaways-fake-an-investigation/. (accessed January 26, 2020).

will always introduce new, innovative tricks to try and hack the system to increase their numbers. However, the follower count displayed on the top of your profile means nothing if it does not correspond to high engagement, loyalty, sales, or (ideally) a potent combination of all three.

Plus, resorting to these last-ditch efforts–whether behind your computer buying robot followers, testing out a follower vending machine in Russia to "see if it works" (wink, wink), or putting a significant amount of cash behind a glorified celebrity sweepstakes–is kind of embarrassing, right? Don't do it.

QUALITY OVER QUANTITY

Alexandra Taylor–SVP of Marketing for Authentic Brands Group (ABG), a brand management and licensing company with a portfolio of over fifty brands from Marilyn Monroe to Juicy Couture–offers a fresh perspective that cautions against placing too much value on follower count. She firmly believes, "It's not about the [number] of followers you have, it's about the quality of those followers and making sure they are the right followers."

When ABG acquired legacy lingerie brand Frederick's of Hollywood, Alexandra and her team discovered that while Frederick's of Hollywood's Instagram account had a healthy following of over 100,000 fans, the number at the top was meaningless from a sales perspective. She explains that "70 percent of [Frederick's of Hollywood's Instagram] followers were male. It took us two years to turn that around to be

70 percent female," which now aligns with who Frederick's of Hollywood's paying customers are–women. Today, the Frederick's of Hollywood Instagram page is in a place where the people who are following the brand and engaging with its content online are the same people making purchases on its website and being loyal to the brand offline, which should be every company's number one priority when it comes to Instagram followers.

At the end of the day, a brand can have millions of followers, but if they are the wrong followers, this seven-figure follower count will not benefit the company in a meaningful manner and will not do anything for the business. Shortcuts can be tempting, and vanity metrics may feel like a quick win up front, but corralling followers instead of building your core business will do nothing for your bottom line, end of story.

You never want to chase the transactional follower. Instead, you want to earn the follower who likes you for you, who will buy what you're selling and tell all their friends about it.

FOLLOWERS DO NOT EQUAL SALES

Let's say you're still not convinced, and you believe that maintaining a large Instagram follower count is the best way for your business to make money.

Take a look at what happened when a popular Instagram influencer attempted to launch her own t-shirt line. Arianna

Renee, known as @Arii to over 2.6 million followers, gave her first t-shirt line the old college try. She designed her shirts, took photos wearing the shirts, and posted them on her Instagram—all standard procedure for an influencer collection. She launched with a limited run of thirty-six units and waited for the sales to come rolling in.

Except they never did.

Arianna was forced to release the following apologetic statement to her 2.6 million Instagram followers:

"Unfortunately, the company that I'm working with goes based on your first drop sales. In order for them to order and make my products (even to keep working with them) I have to sell at least 36 pieces ... No one has kept their word so now the company won't be able to send out the orders to people who actually bought shit and it breaks my heart."

An influencer with 2.6 million followers watching her every move on Instagram could not even sell a mere thirty-six shirts! Thirty-six units of any apparel product isn't that many. You, yes you, could probably make thirty-six shirt sales by the end of the week if you had to, even without 2.6 million people at your fingertips. The adorable lemonade stand on your street corner, manned by a couple of entrepreneurial first graders, likely made more than thirty-six sales over the course of a summer weekend. Does that lemonade stand have the ability to connect with 2.6 million "followers?" I don't think so.

In an article for *Business Insider,* reporter Rachel Hosie finds that @Arii's engagement numbers are consistent with those of fellow mega influencers who have Instagram accounts of similar size, and she confirms that Ari did not attempt to purchase or inflate her follower numbers.[25]

In addition to being truly mind-boggling, the fact that an influencer with 2.6 million followers was unable to sell thirty-six t-shirts proves that maintaining a large Instagram following does not, I repeat, does not correspond to an increase in sales.

---

25 Hosie, Rachel. "An Instagram Star With 2 Million Followers Couldn't Sell 36 T-shirts, and a Marketing Expert Says Her Case isn't Rare." Insider.com. https://www.insider.com/instagrammer-arii-2-million-followers-cannot-sell-36-t-shirts-2019-5. (accessed January 26, 2020).

CHAPTER 11

BUILDING YOUR HOUSE ON SOMEONE ELSE'S LAND

ARTSUGAR

Few industries are as notoriously exclusive and prohibitively expensive as the art world.

Between the exorbitant costs of participating in insider-only auctions, intimidating gatekeepers, and gallery owners who have a reputation for their snobby attitudes, it's no wonder the art market was ripe for a makeover. And what better place to democratize the buying and selling of art than Instagram?

Instagram, a flat, image-centric, free platform, organically hurdles many of the art world's barriers to entry. As Alix Greenberg founded ArtSugar to solve the art world's inherent problems, starting her business as an Instagram-native direct-to-consumer company was the only way to go.

Alix has a traditional art background; she went to art school at Cornell University and earned her masters through Christie's esteemed art program. Starting ArtSugar was Alix's way of breaking from the established art regime and allowing everyday consumers to buy pieces expertly framed at great prices from artists they love and admire. For added sweetness, Alix pairs her artists with a like-minded charity, donating a portion of profits from each sale to a charity of the artists' choosing.

Instagram, in all its visual-first glory, became Alix's social media platform of choice for identifying and connecting with potential customers while showcasing the artists whose work she was selling. Alix recognized that Instagram lends itself to being mutually beneficial for ArtSugar, her featured artists, and the charities receiving donations. As Alix promotes the works of her artists (with Instagram followings from the thousands to well up into the millions), her artists in turn promote ArtSugar as their exclusive point of purchase destination. Both Alix and her artists then promote and give back to a given charitable cause. It's a win-win-win for ArtSugar, the artists, and the philanthropic organizations involved.

In 2018, a whopping 88 percent of ArtSugar's sales came from directly from Instagram. This might seem advantageous at first, because Alix knows exactly how to reach her customers, she has data on who they are and what they like, and they are all instantly accessible with just a few taps on her screen.

Despite the convenience the platform provided ArtSugar, Alix recognized the danger in having her business entirely dependent on Instagram. All of her eggs were in one basket–and worse, she wasn't even the person carrying this metaphorical basket. Yikes.

"I know Instagram isn't going to be around forever, and it's scary to think that I've built my business on this platform that could disappear at any minute," Alix shares, as we discuss the Instagram outages that seem to be increasing in frequency.

INSTAGRAM DOWN

Earlier this spring, Instagram went down for most of the day on multiple occasions. Alix's business was immediately impacted, along with every other brand that chose to post or advertise on Facebook or Instagram that day. Alix felt as if a random team of Instagram engineers had more control over ArtSugar's daily revenue than she did. And worst of all, this particular type of outage affects not just Alix's business, but the artists she represents and philanthropic organizations that depend on her donations.

Entrepreneurs find that the ripple effects of an outage like this are not limited to just that day. When the platform goes down, Instagram does not pay its users back for leads thwarted or revenue lost. Instagram does not reimburse the money you spent on influencer campaigns that went unseen as a result of the outage. If your advertising budget and sales goals are dependent on Instagram, an outage will most certainly decimate your bottom line.

Ashely Carman, writing for *The Verge* on this very topic, details the impact of Instagram's increasing outages: "Millions of companies advertise on the platform or rely on sponsored posts to do the marketing for them. When it goes down, they lose valuable communication lines to the public. Instagram and Facebook are economies unto themselves where people can see advertisements and buy directly from them. The outage is as if billboards and radio ads disappeared from a city, and no one could find the stores where the advertised products are anyway."[26]

Alix had to re-think her business model, and she had to act quickly or risk losing more than she already had. Instead of sitting idle, Alix took action and reevaluated how she was going to hedge against this type of situation–that is wholly out of her control–in the future. She was done advertising on Instagram and instead chose to reallocate the money she would have spent on advertisements back into her business.

Alix used her newfound cash reserve to build out an art rental service that charges a monthly fee to rent ArtSugar pieces

---

26 Carman, Ashley. "When Facebook Goes Down, an Entire Economy Goes Down with It." TheVerge.com. https://www.theverge.com/2019/3/14/18265002/facebook-instagram-outage-ad-revenue-lost. (accessed January 26, 2020).

that can be rotated in and out of your space as often as you choose. As her rental service boomed, Alix became less reliant on Instagram for new customers and could tap into her existing fan base and former buyers for a steady stream of subscription-based revenue. Additionally, she took her marketing efforts offline, partnering with interior designers to get the word out and focusing on non-social-media-based press efforts for her new initiative.

Alix is not giving up on Instagram completely for her business–she is simply recalibrating how she uses it.

Notably, Alix is already thrilled with the results. When a glitch over the summer wouldn't allow her to post anything for four days in a row, she was frustrated, but it was not the end of the world because of her new cash flow model. As it stands, renting is the way of the future, with sustainability a key selling point, so it seems Alix's dynamic approach is ahead of the curve yet again.

The biggest takeaway from speaking with Alix is that founders reliant on Instagram for sales need to start implementing practices for days when Instagram is nonexistent. Or at the very least, they must prepare for a time when it no longer makes sense to allocate your advertising budget and entrepreneurial energy toward the 'Gram.

Alix learned a valuable lesson firsthand–no matter how loyal you are to Instagram, Instagram will not be loyal to you.

BUILDING YOUR DREAM HOUSE

You wouldn't pour your blood, sweat, tears, and all of your money building your dream house (the one with all-marble countertops, a cute little breakfast nook. and a pool out back) on someone else's land, would you? No, because that's a terrible idea! You would have no control over the future of your home, and if the owner decides to sell and force you out, he can! Evicting you is well within his rights as the owner of the land, leaving you and your dream home out to dry.

And when it comes to pouring money into building up your brand account on Instagram, you are building your dream house on someone else's land.

When you're creating your profile, making sure your grid is perfect, spending X amount of dollars to boost each post while running A/B ad campaigns on the backend, you might be thrilled to see your followers, likes, and engagement numbers climbing up, but the problem remains the same: you own none of it. You are renting space from Instagram. You've signed on to let Instagram, a subsidiary of one of the most powerful companies in the world, Facebook, be your landlord.

Scary, right?

As your landlord, Instagram can make changes, big (doing away with a chronological timeline feed) or small (updating its font), as they please, without so much as letting you know.

If Instagram goes down, which users report is happening far more frequently than ever before, you can't call your IT guy to fix it. Instagram will fix it, when its army of engineers gets around to it. Maybe. Hopefully. Eventually. Ultimately, you're stuck dealing with the negative repercussions that Instagram's technical issue has on your business.

When Instagram goes down, a collective panic among users prompts a simultaneous migration to Twitter. On Twitter, users commiserate with like-minded Insta-addicts because, as they say, misery loves company. Jokes and memes are created, shared, and re-shared as users wait for the platform that houses their addiction to be restored to a usable state. Keep in mind this holds true for your everyday Instagram user, even someone whose financial well-being isn't at all tied to Instagram's daily functionality.

However, for the small or even big business owner, just a few hours off of Instagram can be catastrophic for their entire monthly sales goal, and no one is laughing.

IT GETS SCARIER

Aside from the potential monetary loss an Instagram outage poses to your bottom line, what's stopping Instagram from making an update that affects the way you reach your customers?

Nothing!

While it is true that Facebook and Instagram paved the way for businesses to communicate with their customers 'round the clock and at a previously unimaginable scale, it's important to remember they are your landlord when you choose to use their services. You are beholden to their whims and decisions, and you truly have no recourse if their agenda does not line up with yours.

If Instagram changed completely or was gone tomorrow, would you still have access to the customers you're attracting through social media? If the answer is no, you need to adjust your customer acquisition strategy and business model, well, yesterday.

Fortunately for ArtSugar, Alix recognized early that her company was vulnerable due to its over reliance on Instagram. Her foresight kept ArtSugar thriving, and the business will be around for a lot longer than those of entrepreneurs who are willing to turn a blind eye to the details of their unfortunate rental agreement.

CHAPTER 12

THE LANDLORD-TENANT RELATIONSHIP NOBODY WANTS

DAME PRODUCTS

"If you can't join them, sue them" could easily be the unofficial motto of Dame Products' latest marketing campaign.

Dame Products takes a scientific approach to women's health and sexual pleasure. The business makes and sells vibrators with the goal of closing the pleasure gap, or the idea that men orgasm significantly more than women. By all accounts, Dame Products' business is the exact opposite of that seedy, dirty video store that sells sex toys in the back (you know, the one on the corner in the neighborhood you're not so sure you're totally comfortable being in to begin with). And of course, they take significant strides to make sure you never equate the two.

Founded by Alexandra Fine, a Columbia University graduate with a Master of Arts in Clinical Psychology with a concentration in sex therapy, and Janet Lieberman, an engineer from MIT, Dame is all about hard facts and science when it comes to developing its vibrators.[27]

Thanks to extensive research on the female anatomy, Dame's design is sleek, minimalist, and ergonomic. The look and feel of Dame Products' logo and branding, also sleek and minimalist, could be slapped on a consumer product in any industry today (think mattresses, bed linens, toothbrushes—all my favorite examples) and give the impression that the company is smart, sophisticated, and profitable. It has all the typical characteristics of what we deem to be a successful brand in the modern world, especially brands that advertise all over social media.

Yet, due to the sexual nature of the company, Dame Products is routinely blocked from advertising on Facebook and Instagram. Co-founder Alexandra Fine elaborates on Dame's struggles with using Instagram ads: "Facebook and Instagram guidelines, just like anybody's guidelines or policies, are incredibly valuable; however, they have subjective causes and they change them whenever they want. I'm often trying to do things that are within their policy, and then they change the policy to make it not within their policy."

In order to continue marketing her product and stay within the bounds of Facebook's regulations, Alexandra shifted her

---

27 Greco, Alanna. "Dame Sex Toy Company's "Eva" Hands-Free Couple's Vibrator Could Be a Game Changer." Bustle.com. https://www.bustle.com/articles/46437-dame-sex-toy-companys-eva-hands-free-couples-vibrator-could-be-a-game-changer. (accessed January 26, 2020).

company's marketing strategy from promoting her vibrators to promoting herself. Self-promotion is well within the rules of social media. After all, isn't that what having an online presence all about?

All was well until "Facebook decided that *The New York Times* article, the *W Magazine* article, the *BBC* video, and all the content that I was promoting was inappropriate because it showed a vibrator at some point or acknowledged that vibrators exist. [Facebook] changed their policy a little bit [so even my self-promotion was banned]."

A FRUSTRATING REALITY

Alexandra speaks to the frustrations of being a tenant of the world's most arbitrary landlord, Instagram's parent company, Facebook. She knows she will continue to have issues with the platform, despite the fact that any other founder with the same branding, science-backed approach to a universally understood problem and incredible press reach would have no trouble pouring money into social media ads.

Alexandra kept altering Dame's advertising approach to no avail. Instead of specifically promoting her company's vibrators, she put resources toward pushing Dame's sex accessories on the platform, and she worked with a Facebook specialist to ensure the company's ads would be well within Facebook's guidelines.

"Recently we got [Facebook] ads working for our lubricants and our positioning pillow. I worked directly with Facebook to make this happen. They said that [our ads] were fine. And they were working successfully for a few weeks, until Facebook came down on us and took them down."

At the end of the day, founders like Alexandra have no recourse when this happens. She can never get back the time she spent creating the at-one-time approved ads. She can never recover the resources spent on creating and implementing the ads, like her creative direction, graphic design, and photography budgets. For founders like Alexandra, attempting to game the system, or even work within the system, often proves to be a lost cause.

Alexandra's frustrations are valid. She elaborates, "I set out to do something that I thought was going to better the world and I knew that it might be taboo, but I thought that as long as I'm presenting science and facts and data that I could help people understand, but apparently to companies and institutions like Facebook, science doesn't matter."

I asked Alexandra if she was planning to continue investing in Facebook ads and she confirmed that she won't be for the time being. Instead, she's refocusing her efforts on other things–a completely understandable approach to a problem that for her, and companies like hers, has no good solution when renting space on someone else's land.

TAKING HER DOLLARS ELSEWHERE

Alexandra understood the value of diversifying her advertising channels, so she had been simultaneously working on a New York

City subway takeover marketing campaign when her issues with social media surfaced. Given the Metropolitan Transit Authority's (MTA) advertising partnership with Hims, essentially a millennial-targeted Viagra, Alexandra assumed Dame would encounter little to no resistance launching its subway ad campaign.

Previously, Hims ran a (not-so-subtle) subway takeover campaign featuring pictures of cactuses in the shape of erect penises on the walls and turnstiles of busy subway stops.

To ensure Dame's ad campaign would meet the MTA's politically correct regulations, Alexandra worked directly with representatives from the government agency to create advertisements that were both on-brand for her company and appropriate per the MTA's standards.

Despite the precautions Alexandra had taken, and after months of good-natured collaboration, *Buzzfeed* notes, "in December 2018, the MTA unexpectedly denied the [Dame Products'] request [to advertise], citing new additions to its advertisement policies as seen on its Frequently Asked Questions page. 'The MTA Advertising Policy prohibits any advertisement that promotes a 'sexually oriented business,'' the page reads, noting that 'advertisements for sex toys or devices for any gender fall within this category.'"[28]

28 Vu, Nancy. "These Women are Suing to Let New York Subway Riders See Their Vibrators." Buzzfeednews.com. https://www.buzzfeednews.com/article/nancyvu/dame-sex-toy-company-sue-nyc-mta. (accessed January 26, 2020).

Understandably, this message came as a shock to Alexandra and to Dame Products, which stated in its lawsuit that it had spent "approximately $150,000 of its scant resources to incorporate the MTA's feedback, submit revised advertisements, and order additional inventory, all in reliance on the MTA's representation that it would accept Dame's materials." The company had submitted various rounds of edited advertisements to the MTA, but the final version was ultimately rejected because the MTA had labelled Dame as a "sexually orientated business, which has long been prohibited by the MTA's advertising standards."

Hmm...sounds familiar.

IF YOU CAN'T BEAT THEM, SUE THEM

Alexandra chose to sue the MTA for gender-based discrimination.

She formally filed a freedom of speech violation against the MTA on the basis that it had willingly approved a male-oriented, sexually charged marketing campaign for subway advertisements while denying the same opportunity to a female-focused company offering similar products.

With the lawsuit came an onslaught of press and an outpouring of support for Alexandra and Dame Products.

As a marketing bonus, the lawsuit and subsequent press coverage introduced millions of new potential customers to the brand. As far as Alexandra is concerned, the results "have been great." In our conversation, Alexandra continued to note that embracing the press from the lawsuit, including multiple *New York Times* pieces (one titled, "Vaginas Deserve Giant Ads, Too" and another, "Sex Sells, but When It Comes to Female Pleasure, the New York Subway Isn't So Sure"), "is much smarter and better than just being upset that they wouldn't let us run ads, and I definitely am getting a lot more out of the work that I did by creating a story by suing them. In that respect, it's been a great marketing campaign."

Lawsuits are inherently expensive, so it is typically the kiss of death for a startup to be engaged in an ongoing lawsuit in its nascent years. Yet, for Dame Products, the lawsuit against the MTA provides the company with the opportunity to take a public stand against institutionalized sexism, which happens to align perfectly with the company's core message and brand ideals. Though a marketing professor or a startup whiz would never advocate for a company to enter a lawsuit for the sole purpose of brand exposure, Dame Products' legal rights were infringed upon and it would be foolish not to take action and capitalize on such an organic marketing opportunity at the same time.

MAKING SENSE OF IT ALL

Working within a set of guidelines that is subject to change at any moment is one of the biggest drawbacks of businesses relying on a single channel of advertising. Unfortunately, due to the nature of her product, Alexandra saw firsthand how sexism came into play when she tried to branch out from her digital ad strategy and do a subway takeover. But crafting a narrative around her pain points while having a valid chance at winning the lawsuit has allowed her to take the power back.

For Dame Products, organic marketing strategies and viral conversation starters are more worthwhile (and far more valuable) than hoping and praying Facebook and the MTA will one day decide to miraculously change their opaque and user-unfriendly policies. Better yet, the new customers Dame has attracted with its lawsuit are not simply purchasing the company's products and carrying on with their lives. Instead, the customers have become loyal fans who truly believe in Dame's gender equality mission and are willing to rally behind the cause.

If the Marketing Funnel has taught us anything, it's that people who are willing to advocate on behalf of your brand are far more valuable to a company than those one-time purchasers who click "buy" after coming across a digital ad. Furthermore, fans who were drawn to the brand by the onslaught of lawsuit-related press will be the people who help fund this lawsuit, both indirectly (by purchasing Dame's products) and directly (by donating to Dame's legal fee fund on its website).

When I spoke candidly with Alexandra about the discrimination she and her company have faced when attempting to advertise both on Facebook and with the MTA, she reveals that "one of the main reasons why we decided to [sue the MTA] is because I do think it could be the beginning of a precedent for us to be able to make a case against Facebook."

If the court of public opinion has anything to say about it, Alexandra and Dame Products will have even more widespread support when they do take on Facebook.

FREE THE NIPPLE

When I noticed that some of my Just Nips Instagram posts and advertisements had been flagged and taken down, I thought it simply must be a mistake. A clear accident. An obvious oversight on Facebook's part.

Intentionally, I never posted overtly sexual content on the Just Nips Instagram account because I knew Facebook had been waging war on women's nipples for years, beginning with the highly publicized #FreeTheNipple battle.

For context, the #FreeTheNipple controversy began in 2013 when activist Lina Esco filmed a documentary about herself running through the streets topless. She posted clips of her work on Facebook, which Facebook abruptly removed from its platform. Public outcry over the censorship ensued and celebrities like Miley Cyrus, Lena Dunham, Chelsea Handler, Rihanna, and Chrissy Teigen took to the cause, posting pictures of themselves topless to show their support, though Facebook remained unmoved.[29] Today, the matter remains unresolved, with the latest iteration of the saga allowing the male nipple to be displayed on Instagram while the female nipple is still decidedly banned.

After watching this drama unfold right before launching Just Nips, I knew I would need to proceed with caution when posting content on Facebook and Instagram. By design, when it came to Just Nips creative, nary a nipple was in sight! The outline of a nipple, as seen from the outside of a woman's shirt, yes. But an actual female nipple? No.

For Mother's Day, Just Nips attempted to promote a video on Facebook and Instagram featuring testimonials from women in the breast cancer community who had purchased our medical-grade nipple enhancers. The video in question featured animated quotes from happy customers against a polka dotted background. It was short, to the point, admittedly on the boring side, and as PG as could be.

Of course, Facebook felt differently and proceeded to flag the video and remove it from my feed.

I wrote into the Facebook "help" portal far more times than I would like to admit. I did everything I could to get answers to no avail. In hindsight, I cannot believe I was naive enough to believe I would receive a meaningful response.

---

29 "Wikipedia: Free the Nipple (campaign)." Wikimedia Foundation, last modified January 25, 2020. https://en.wikipedia.org/wiki/Free_the_Nipple_(campaign).

In an unsurprising turn of events, it appears Facebook did not *accidentally* remove Just Nips' posts and ads from its platform. Just Nips' association with nipples in any capacity was very much the problem. And that was that. Just Nips' ability to promote anything on Facebook and Instagram was gone.

WHOSE BUSINESS IS IT ANYWAY?

In hindsight, the issue was never that I was "right" and Facebook was "wrong." It wasn't about Facebook being intentionally opaque, too politically correct, or even "unfair."

The root of the issue was that Facebook and Just Nips are separate businesses with different, non-overlapping goals, key performance indicators, and revenue models.

Facebook is in the business of selling advertisements. Just Nips and other product-based brands are in the business of selling product. Facebook's profits are driven by the number and scope of ads *it* sells. The profits of product-based brands are driven by the number of units *they* sell.

With this in mind, Facebook isn't going to waste the valuable time of its sales team helping "controversial" companies purchase ads when it can better utilize its sales team and considerable resources selling ads to less problematic businesses.

When you boil it down, more businesses want to advertise on Facebook than there are social media platforms available for companies to effectively advertise on. It would be negligent for Facebook not to use this to its advantage when optimizing its sales and customer support strategies.

Now that we have all that squared away, you might be wondering how Facebook treats product-based brands that are not deemed "controversial."

Let's go back to my fake startup, TEETHbrshs. As the owner of TEETHbrshs, I recognize the injustices and inherent sexism companies like Dame Products and Just Nips have experienced on Facebook and am empathetic to their causes. But I, too, have a business to run and I'm taking my marketing dollars to Facebook.

At first glance, I, like many in my shoes, will argue that if my product-based business chooses to run advertisements on Facebook, both TEETHbrshs and Facebook's business goals will, in fact, be aligned. I give them money; they give me exposure. But that would assume that both parties are entering a mutually respectful agreement, which is not at all the case.

When TEETHbrshs chooses to advertise on Facebook, it agrees to a rental agreement in which it is the tenant and Facebook is the landlord. Nowhere in the "lease agreement" does Facebook state that it cares about the profits of its tenants, or that it will try to help tenants like TEETHbrshs maximize their profits. At the end of the day, Facebook does not care how many units you sell. Facebook only cares about how many advertisements Facebook sells.

In other words, your return on investment from your ad spend with Facebook means a hell of a lot more to you than it does to Facebook. No matter how you spin it, this arrangement is always going to be more beneficial for the landlord than for the tenant. After all, the tenant pays the landlord at the end of every month, no matter how many units of product the tenant sells. A paid advertisement is guaranteed revenue for Facebook. A paid advertisement for TEETHbrshs guarantees nothing more than exposure (and the quality of the exposure is another factor up for debate). It's bait on the end of a fishing pole. Sometimes you catch a big fish, and sometimes you starve.

Holy mackerel! If you happen to find yourself with a landlord who demonstrates Facebook-like tendencies, move—and move fast.

A DEAL WITH THE DEVIL

When dealing with Facebook, the world's worst landlord, smaller companies (i.e., almost every other company on the planet) truly have no recourse. When the platform decides to make changes that negatively impact the accounts of some small businesses or when it chooses to enact arbitrary regulations that cripple a few more small businesses, the owners of these companies are blindsided and left picking up the pieces with nothing to show for their efforts or ad spend.

Alexandra Fine's fierce resolve to land on her feet after Facebook and the MTA pulled the rug out from underneath Dame

Products is why her company is thriving today. Alexandra's willingness to turn lemons into lemonade by suing the MTA for gender discrimination resulted in more positive publicity than Dame Products could likely have ever afforded through traditional marketing or PR channels. In most situations, going head to head with Facebook is simply not worth it, but Alexandra has found a way to spin the challenge into an opportunity to grow her business while benefiting women across the world.

Advertising on Facebook is the ultimate Faustian bargain. If you're unfamiliar with the legend of Faust, his tragic tale goes like this: Faust was a successful man who was unsatisfied with his life. In exchange for short-term knowledge and pleasure, Faust sold his soul to the devil, despite knowing from the get-go this would turn out poorly for him in the long run. Unsurprisingly, this agreement did not end well for Faust, who ended up in hell, more miserable than ever before.

Brands who are attracted to the short-term benefits of purchasing ads on Facebook and Instagram willingly enter into a deal with the devil if they plan to rely solely on these social media platforms for growth.

CHAPTER 13

THE ICEBERG FILTER

THE POWER OF INSTAGRAM

In a book all about Instagram, it would be negligent to gloss over the power of Instagram as a business tool and its ability to ability to connect buyers to sellers, grow brands, and sell products.

Interestingly enough, many of the entrepreneurs I interview in this book would not be entrepreneurs if it weren't for Instagram. Instagram provided these entrepreneurs with the opportunity to post something they had created and were proud of with the ability to receive real-time feedback from the market that hey, people will actually spend their money on this thing I made!

Instagram has played a pivotal role in promoting some of the most successful brands we see on our feeds today. Here are some examples.

Jars by Dani: Colorful cake creations layered with gooey frosting and rainbow sprinkles, adorably packed inside a mason jar double as the perfect serving size and the ideal subject for an Instagram post. Jars by Dani, an innovative (and profitable) dessert company got its start all because of Instagram. Founder Dani Beckerman explains, "I started my business by accident through Instagram. I put up a post six-plus years ago and people immediately started to reach out and ask if they could buy [my Jars] ... it's insane that it all grew from there. Instagram really allowed me to get the word out. I attribute a ton of my success to Instagram." Thanks to the power of Instagram, Dani was able to successfully transform a single post into a full-fledged business.

Frank Body: People do crazy things for the 'Gram, like covering their faces with coffee grinds and posting a photo for proof. However, not just any old coffee grinds will do, the ones that *really* go viral are produced by Frank Body, a Melbourne-based beauty company credited with starting and perpetuating the coffee bean face mask Insta-trend.

The team behind Frank Body, a twenty-million-dollar business that began with one product, a coffee body scrub, has also been vocal about its reliance on Instagram to grow the business to where it is today. "We launched with a very humble budget ... We wouldn't have the business we have today had it not been for our ability to leverage platforms like Instagram and Facebook" co-founder Jess Hatzis tells Forbes.[30] Frank

30 Decker, Vivienne. "How Australia's Frank Body Built a $20 Million Global Beauty Brand on Social Media." Forbes.com. https://www.forbes.com/sites/viviennedecker/2017/02/22/how-australias-frank-body-built-a-20m-global-beauty-brand-on-social-media/#3a84d6814709. (accessed January 26, 2020).

Body has been able to grow, expand, and reach international markets at record speeds, thanks to the virality of user-generated content featuring its products.

Stoney Clover Lane: What started out as two teenage sisters making bracelets together for fun turned into the popular accessories line slash Instagram sensation, Stoney Clover Lane. All of Stoney Clover Lane's products feature dazzling colors, patterns, and customizable monograms that practically beg people to post them.

With sales in the "high seven figures,"[31] many cite the Stoney Clover Lane Instagram account as a key sales driver for the brand. It is. Though, what's more impressive is the way Stoney Clover Lane utilizes Instagram as a touchpoint and research tool. The company relies on Instagram to connect with its customers and to learn about their likes and dislikes so it can tailor new products to its fans' specific preferences. Additionally, thanks to Instagram, the Stoney Clover Lane team had its finger on the pulse of Gen-Z shopping habits long before many of its competitors even realized Gen-Z was an important demographic to target.

Briogeo: I asked a few friends if they had ever heard of the clean haircare line Briogeo and they all said some variation of, "Yes, it's the shampoo from Something Navy!" Of course, they are all referring to mega-influencer Arielle Charnas, known for her long, wavy hair and lifestyle blog titled Something Navy.

---

31 Richards, Kate. "How Stoney Clover Lane Marries DTC and Physical Stores." Glossy.com. https://www.glossy.co/fashion/how-stoney-clover-lane-marries-dtc-and-physical-stores. (accessed January 26, 2020).

After Arielle posted her shower routine on Instagram a few times, fans were quick to take note of Briogeo Shampoo, one of her most-used products, and ran out to purchase it for themselves. Thanks to all the love on Instagram, many fans associate the Briogeo haircare startup with giving Arielle her signature hairstyle, which is particularly ironic considering Arielle herself was the face of a previous commercial endorsement with legacy haircare line TRESemmé years before.

REMOVING THE FILTER

It's easy to attribute the lasting success of these brands solely to their presence on Instagram, but hopefully you now understand why that would be an oversimplification.

Jars by Dani, Frank Body, Stoney Clover Lane, and Briogeo have all found ways to make Instagram work for them, but that's just half the story.

While these brands have certainly leveraged Instagram to their advantage, each has also made strategic business decisions behind the scenes that are just as important to their success. The success stories above are filtered versions of their businesses—the tip of the iceberg, if you will.

By removing the glossy, high-resolution filter from each brand, we find:

Jars by Dani employed strategic partnerships from the start, scoring a transformational partnership with billion-dollar conglomerate Unilever after just a few years in business.

Frank Body groomed wholesale relationships for years, and you can find its products in difficult-to-break-into retailers like Urban Outfitters, Ulta, and Bloomingdales.

Stoney Clover Lane has been all about retail, with outposts in Palm Beach, New York City, and East Hampton. It has also dabbled in successful popups and collaborations, notably with fellow Instagram-darling brand LoveShackFancy and another with jewelry line, Lele Sadoughi ... and that's just in the past year alone.

Briogeo's success proves you can be an influencer's favorite hair line and still have more traditionally understood business wins like a multi-year placement in Sephora, the undisputed holy grail of beauty retail.

MOVING ON

The next part of *The Instagram Iceberg* delves beneath the surface to reveal what takes place beyond the tip of the iceberg at some of your favorite Instagram-friendly companies. My goal is to remove the filter and provide you with the unedited version (sans FaceTune) of how successful companies have built their brands.

I will also explain how the most progressive and forward-thinking companies are priming their businesses for a day without Instagram, and how you can, too.

CHAPTER 14

THINK INSIDE THE BOX

BLOOMSCAPE

Justin Mast was at a loss when it came to combatting the rising costs of customer acquisition for his startup, Bloomscape.

So, he called his mom for help.

Bloomscape is a direct-to-consumer company that delivers luscious, thriving plants straight from the greenhouse to your doorstep. Bloomscape, like so many companies in this highly competitive digital landscape, wasn't loving (to put it nicely) the high price of customer acquisition on social media that only seemed to be rising.

Justin's mom didn't have any experience in the startup world, but that didn't stop her from becoming a key strategic factor in strengthening Bloomscape's bottom line. Justin's mom became a winning solution for a customer acquisition cost problem that, at a time, felt like it could never be solved.

Justin founded Bloomscape in 2018, but his family history in the botany business goes way back. On his dad's side, Justin's family has been in the greenhouse industry for five generations while his mom's side of the family has been involved in the floral industry for three. Justin grew up learning all about what it takes to run a successful plant business using the traditional model that had been used for decades.

That said, he had some frustrations with the way plants were previously delivered to consumers. Often, florists delivered plants in trucks with uncontrolled climates or kept the plants in dark warehouses for weeks at a time before finally delivering them to their new homes. These logistical failings left the customer with unhealthy plants, but, as with most industries ripe for disruption, this was the way it had been done for years, so the business model stuck.

Justin wasn't always sure he wanted to work in the industry he grew up in, but he had an idea for a company that would deliver plants in pristine condition to customers who cared just as much as he did about the benefits of bringing greenery into the home. This was one of those ideas that would keep him awake in the middle of the night. Knowing he had enough industry knowledge about plant supply chains, where the gaps were, and how to fix them himself, Justin set off to do just that.

When it came time to launch Bloomscape, Justin notes that he was planning to stick with the Glossier and Casper playbook of driving high growth through online advertising, which in his words was "raising a ton of venture capital and digital marketing the crap out of [your company]." But Facebook had other plans, and in light of the Cambridge Analytica election scandal that took place two months after Bloomscape's launch, Facebook removed its particular Audience Insights tool that was key to their strategy.

Justin elaborates, "Facebook pulled [their Audience Insights tool] right when we launched, and we were bummed out because we were really excited to learn how to really capture our audience and learn as much as possible about them. We were so hungry for information. I learned quickly that Facebook is great when it's great, but it can change overnight."

Justin took the setback in stride and welcomed the opportunity to not become too reliant on one marketing channel. And that's when he called his mom, Joyce.

Throughout his life, any time Justin had a question, comment, or concern about one of his household plants, he would text his mom a picture and she would come back with a course of action: move it a little to the left, turn it ninety degrees so it's out of direct sunlight, water it with lukewarm water only—and voila! His plant would thrive.

Justin wanted to bring his mom's botanical expertise to his one-hundred-thousand-plus customers but understood the limitations of trying to scale a single person's unique skill set. Nevertheless, he had to start somewhere, so Joyce became

Bloomscape's official Plant Mom. Bloomscape's decision to install and market around Plant Mom proved to be a winning strategy on multiple fronts.

Plant Mom was immediately inundated with thousands of emails and texts from Bloomscape customers who sought her expert advice about keeping their plants healthy. Shortly after, Bloomscape added a content marketing strategy into the rotation with Joyce's horticulture expertise at the helm. Today, Bloomscape has an entire Green Team dedicated to helping out Plant Mom by fielding inquiries and keeping the lines of communication open with its customers.

A UNIQUE DIGITAL EXPERIENCE

The strategy behind Plant Mom works for a multitude of reasons. Initially, when you learn about Plant Mom, her role within the company doesn't feel like a marketing tactic. Customers are brought into the Bloomscape universe and greeted by the founder's mom, who just so happens to have years of horticulture experience under her belt coupled with an inherently nurturing demeanor that is so authentic, it translates seamlessly from offline to online.

By sharing best practices from her years of experience, not just in the floral industry but from being a committed plant owner herself, Plant Mom is able to calm the nerves of first-time plant parents who are anxious about doing something wrong at best and killing their plants at worst.

If any of Bloomscape's customers pick up on the irony that is purchasing a plant online to fulfill a desire to be more connected to planet Earth, Plant Mom offers the grounded connection they craved from the start.

Plant Mom is a digital experience anchored by its uniquely human touch, which is why it is so successful as a marketing tool. Bringing Plant Mom into the marketing mix adds to the customer experience, on top of serving as a stellar talking point (can you think of a more wholesome word-of-mouth sales driver?) and a way to keep customers coming back for more.

If your takeaway from Bloomscape's Plant Mom ploy is to call your mom and get her involved in your marketing strategy, you're missing the point. Plant Mom works for Bloomscape because it naturally adds a personal touch to a product that is particularly personal–a plant for your home.

When brainstorming ways to incorporate a new experience into your business to boost customer acquisition, or any facet of your business for that matter, you must search for angles inside your company that are the perfect balance of synergistic (i.e., beneficial for both your business and your customers) and additive to your business, like Bloomscape and Plant Mom. And remember, taking inventory of the resources you already have will often times yield better results than trying to come up with the next big thing and backing it into your existing business goals.

THE BEST PART!

Justin is open about the fact that the cost of acquiring new customers on Facebook and Instagram has increased by two to three times since Bloomscape launched, which he chalks up to the routine cost of doing business on the platform.

While Bloomscape doesn't rely 100 percent on Instagram for customer acquisition, it is still active on the platform and has cultivated a loyal and engaged audience. Justin explains, "It's never been about 'How do we have a great Instagram strategy;' instead, it's 'How do we have a big customer conversation, and when is Instagram the best place to do that?'" Bloomscape seamlessly integrates its Plant Mom initiative into its Instagram strategy only when it fits and makes the most sense. For the full Plant Mom experience, your best bet is contacting her directly.

My favorite takeaway from Bloomscape's implementation of its Plant Mom strategy is that it replaced the startup's need to be reliant on Facebook for consumer data. The data and customer information Justin was initially disappointed to lose out on when Facebook removed its Audience Insights tool was right in his mom's email inbox the entire time. From the thousands of email exchanges between Plant Mom and Bloomscape customers, Justin and his team learned more about his customers' preferences than he ever could have from a Facebook tool.

LESSONS LEARNED

The story of Plant Mom demonstrates why creativity will always trump following the herd or waiting around for Facebook to change course.

Additionally, the reason the Plant Mom strategy is so effective is because it seamlessly integrates the values that plant-purchasing consumers are drawn to in the first place. Bloomscape's way of conducting business resonates with the homey, down-to-Earth, mother-nature-like experience that its consumers seek when buying plants, that is otherwise nonexistent when going the online route.

Customers know that when they purchase a plant from Bloomscape, they are getting the real deal. Perhaps most importantly, Bloomscape's story proves yet again why you should always call your mom!

CHAPTER 15

STRATEGIC DIVERSIFICATION

JAJA TEQUILA

Jaja Tequila is in on the joke.

Founded by Instagram mega-influencer @FuckJerry, born Elliot Tebele, his brother Maurice Tebele, and Martin Hoffstein, Jaja Tequila fuses the Millennial penchant for #relatable memes and tequila.

Co-founder Elliot Tebele has been a fixture on Instagram since he started his comedic meme account in April 2011 and became one of the first to realize, understand, and seize the opportunity to build a loyal audience on the platform. The revolutionary style in which Elliot curated his posts and positioned his account paved the way for how we consume content on Instagram today.

Despite the massive success of its founders, the Jaja Tequila brand embraces the self-deprecating side of newfound internet fame. This light-hearted approach is evident in all aspects of the brand's business–from its hilarious marketing tactics to its logo, a bootleg rip-off of the logo used by the 'real' celebrity George Clooney-backed tequila brand, Casamigos.

With Jaja Tequila's network reaching close to fifty million across various online platforms, you wouldn't think twice if the brand chose to market and advertise exclusively on social media.

In fact, it would make sense, almost *too* much sense. It would be a layup for this viral meme of a tequila company to rely solely on its online fan base to scale, generate sales, and stay in their lane, never exploring alternate paths to profitability outside of the Internet.

A hypothetical digital-only campaign would look something like this: @FuckJerry and associated accounts would encourage their followers to go to clubs and bars where Jaja Tequila is sold, order some tequila and tag @Jaja while doing something. Maybe it's a "challenge," albeit a less noble challenge than say, the Ice Bucket Challenge that went viral in 2016 while promoting awareness and raising money for Lou Gehrig's disease, but a challenge nonetheless to get people talking. The more people who partake, the more people who buy Jaja and the more leverage the Jaja team has when trying to introduce its brand to additional restaurants, bars, and stores.

Fans-turned-Jaja-customers wouldn't bat an eyelash if this type of content was clogging their feeds. Not that Jaja's founders are unfamiliar with controversy (Elliot's firm, Jerry Media was at the center of the messy Fyre Festival debacle), but an added bonus of this type of campaign is that it wouldn't break any of the strict rules and regulations of alcohol sales promotion on Instagram.

Instead of opting for the path of least resistance and the digitally exclusive route, however, Jaja Tequila chose to take the decidedly analog out-of-home advertising path instead, erecting a massive billboard in downtown New York City.

The billboard itself says in silly, on-brand, messy handwriting, "Jaja's Marketing Budget," and features a pie chart with a 95 percent-5 percent split, designed to showcase how Jaja is spending its money to market this tequila. An arrow points to the largest portion of the pie that says, "this billboard" with the other arrow pointing to the teeny, tiny sliver of a section and says, "influencer marketing."

Riffing on the fact that they are known as a digitally native tequila company and are social media influencers themselves, this billboard shows even the powers that be behind Jaja Tequila recognize the value in marketing offline for a change.

Co-founder Martin Hoffstein elaborates on Jaja's billboard strategy. "Billboards have become almost like the notch on your belt of success [for a company]. A lot of the billboards that [other brands] put out are a little pretentious or too elevated and certainly not as fun and creative. With Jaja being such a light-hearted brand, we wanted to experiment with out-of-home [advertising] in a way that created more of a fun experience, bringing the humor that we're pushing on digital to real life."

Bridging the gap between the offline and online worlds allows Jaja to reach more people than it would on social media alone. However, the true value comes from the manner in which Jaja extends its playful and punny digital presence into the real world time after time.

After posting a photoshopped ice cream truck featuring the Jaja logo on its Instagram page, the Jaja team was surprised to receive an outpouring of positive feedback from fans commenting that a Jaja tequila truck would make for the perfect brand extension. So, Jaja bought a truck, painted it in the brand's signature colors and hit the road as a full-service (kind of) tequila bar.

When speaking about their strategy, co-founder Maurice Tebele states, "We're super excited to now show how a picture that we posted as almost a joke has become this reality. And that's really what the brand is all about—having fun, connecting with an audience, and being different and not like everyone else."[32]

---

32 Hogan, Cara. "The Empowered Marketer: Maurice Tebele and Martin Hoffstein of JAJA Tequila." Zaius.com. https://www.zaius.com/learn/the-empowered-marketer-jaja-tequila/. (accessed January 26, 2020).

Additionally, Jaja has continued to explore options in the out-of-home advertising space with guerrilla marketing campaigns featuring wheat paste posters all over New York City. On social, the brand issued a call to action to its social media followers encouraging them to snap their own pictures of Jaja ads out in the wild for a chance to win a free trip to Mexico. Here, Jaja Tequila is leveraging both the power of traditional advertising campaigns and their robust social media following to increase their impact.

Jaja Tequila's marketing tactics are applied both online and offline. Fittingly, while "Jaja jaja jaja" is not exactly a literal Spanish to English translation for laughing all the way to the bank, it is close enough to make it work.

HYBRID MARKETING

As opposed to those who skew too heavily toward an Instagram-specific advertising approach, businesses that choose to harness the power of both online and offline marketing strategies set themselves up for long-term commercial success.

Most importantly, incorporating other strategies alongside your social media efforts is the best way to mitigate your downside, should one of your strategies fail to yield the desired results. It speaks to a growing trend in marketing that engages more than just one advertising channel at a time: strategic diversification.

CLOVE SHOES

Happy wife, happy life. Great words to live by, right? However, Clove founder Joe Ammon's wife, Tamara, was not happy at all. Tamara's feet were killing her!

After working long nursing shifts at the hospital, Tamara would come home and complain about her uncomfortable shoes. She had yet to find a shoe she could wear to work that provided adequate support, comfort, and the style she deserved. Tamara was constantly buying and trying new shoes to no avail. Nothing on the market seemed to meet her specific needs.

So, Joe took matters into his own hands. Joe did his research and developed a shoe designed specifically for healthcare professionals. Clove shoes are made with unique materials that are liquid repellent, are stain resistant, and feature anti-odor insoles. They are tough enough to keep up with the demands of twenty-four-hour wear cycles and fashionable enough to rock sans scrubs.

One look at Clove's Instagram page tells you this brand emphasizes both form *and* function. It features stylized photography that is a nod to the needs of its target demographic: healthcare providers. Clove's copy astutely portrays healthcare providers as unsung heroes and speaks to the uncommon demands of the medical industry in an approachable and relatable manner. From a social media marketing standpoint, Clove is doing everything right.

In speaking to the benefits of leveraging social media to spread the word about Clove, Joe notes that the healthcare community is particularly active on Instagram. The platform hosts an entire ecosystem of people who can relate to the grueling hours and unique demands of the job while providing a welcome means of social connection when no one else is awake.

Armed with an insider's view of the healthcare industry, Joe was more than prepared to advertise on Instagram when it came time to launch his company.

After noticing the onslaught of flattering press touting the revolutionary nature of Clove shoes, the head of the New York Professional Nurses Union (NYPNU) reached out to Joe to explore partnership options. Joe jumped at the opportunity to offer a meaningful 10 percent discount on Clove shoes to all nurses who were members of the NYPNU.

After a successful campaign, Joe tapped into other nursing unions around the country to offer the same discount and attract new customers. Before he knew it, Joe had access to over forty thousand nurses.

Meanwhile, Clove was successfully targeting nurses on Instagram, with a customer acquisition cost of approximately twenty-five dollars per new customer. Given that a pair of Clove shoes retails for $129, a customer acquisition cost that is less than 20 percent of the unit's retail price is quite impressive. On the other side of the equation, Clove has managed to drop its offline customer acquisition cost to an astounding thirteen dollars per new customer.

As a new company, it would have been easy for Clove to allocate all of its advertising budget toward one promotional channel and hope for the best. Yet, Joe and his team at Clove appreciate the unique opportunities for growth available through a marketing strategy that incorporates both online and offline promotion. Had Clove been too laser-focused on an expensive Instagram advertising campaign, it might have missed a golden opportunity to partner with the NYPNU and gain access to over forty thousand prospective customers.

STRATEGIC DIVERSIFICATION

Throughout this book, we have explored various examples of offline marketing strategies yielding strong results for companies entering the retail race. That said, there is certainly a time and a place to justify an investment in Instagram advertising, especially when the investment is necessary to fuel growth. The key is tapping into complementary on and offline marketing initiatives to discover points of synergy on behalf of your brand.

Allocating marketing spend across multiple successful strategies will only improve your bottom line. However, implementing a diversified approach such as Clove's use of strategic partnerships, traditional press efforts, and Instagram ads is a simple yet successful strategy that often leads to super additive value creation.

Both Jaja Tequila and Clove's approaches to strategic diversification prove that when it comes to marketing, the whole is greater than the sum of its parts.

CHAPTER 16

GO WHERE YOUR CUSTOMERS ARE

SUSAN ALEXANDRA

Susan Korn was the luckiest Bat Mitzvah girl in the world.

Her party was everything a girl could want for a celebration marking her coming of age. Better yet, Susan was able to have complete creative control throughout every step of the event planning process. She was unlike most Bat Mitzvah girls whose moms allow their daughters one trip to the party planner as more of a feel-good formality than an opportunity for actual input.

As such, Susan brought her vision to life: an over-the-top explosion of pink balloons and sparkly streamers covering every inch of the seventeenth floor of the Public Hotel, complete with 360-degree views of New York City, a view guests could enjoy if they could poke their heads through the never-ending sea of sparkles, streamers, and glitter!

Best of all, Susan was allowed to wear whatever she wanted (a typically catastrophic point of contention during the Bat Mitzvah lead-up) to mark the occasion, and she chose a lime green butterfly crop top with matching lime green pants.

When it came time for the guest list, Susan had no parent-imposed limit and invited all her friends and all her 150,000 "friends" from Instagram to celebrate with her.

At the ripe age of thirty-four, Susan's Bat Mitzvah was more than just a coming-of-age celebration for her (she'd already had her "real" Bat Mitzvah twenty-one years earlier), but also her handbag, accessories, and fashion line, Susan Alexandra.

It's easy to see how Susan and her wares became cult favorites among the fashion crowd. Susan herself is just as bubbly as the products in her namesake line. In the otherwise dark and stuffy world of fashion, Susan has been able to carve out an impressive and unique niche that is representative of her bright, happy self.

All of Susan's creations are loud, kitschy, and inherently spark joy. In other words, they fit right in with her Bat Mitzvah decor, which is the point.

THE ULTIMATE INSTAGRAM-OPTIMIZED MARKETING EXPERIENCE, BUT MAKE IT FASHION

Susan's Bat Mitzvah party was a way for Susan and her fashion line to partake in the hubbub of Fashion Week but to do so on her terms.

The traditional runway shows that dominate Fashion Week offer brands a simple, streamlined opportunity to showcase their latest styles to editors, buyers, and recently, the general public. As a tradeoff, the shows tend to follow a strict schedule with rigid seating charts and a particular (if not peculiar) way of doing things.

"It's a big milestone for brands to have their first traditional runway show, but I don't feel a connection with that style of fashion show," Susan says of the current fashion show expectations. Instead of pushing tortured models down a catwalk–a cookie cutter variation of what everyone else does–Susan opted to host an event that was authentically true to her vision.

The Bat Mitzvah was more than just a way to partake in Fashion Week; it was an ode to the growth and maturity of her company over the last few years. And of course, Susan's Bat Mitzvah was Instagram-friendly. Think: sparkly streamers, bountiful balloons, colorful confetti, and a celebratory hora dance.

While scrolling through their feeds during Fashion Week, the entire fashion world was seeing the same old catwalk after catwalk. Susan's Bat Mitzvah broke the mold and offered a rare glimpse into something unique, authentic and decidedly on-brand during a week when most brands wouldn't dare deviate from the norm.

It's important to note that Susan's Bat Mitzvah wasn't just Instagram-optimized for the sake of increasing likes and engagement on social media. The party was Instagram-optimized because that is part of Susan's and, by extension, her brand's aesthetic. Every single part of the Bat Mitzvah made strategic sense, including its "like-able," share-able vibe.

WHY IT WORKS

Susan attributes much of her company's success to Instagram, touting it as the "best way to make connections with my customers." She notes, "I don't know what I would be doing if I didn't have Instagram!"

In a profile piece on *Manrepeller* titled, "Inside The Endearing Cult of Susan Alexandra," Susan's Head of Photo encapsulates her Insta-appeal: "Susan can relate to her customers on a personal level through Instagram, sharing memes, answering DMs and comments, and posting daily as if she was just another girl next door."[33] In other words, Susan comes off as your best friend who just so happens to sell stuff and be Insta-famous at the same time.

---

33 Ross, Harling. "Inside the Endearing Cult of Susan Alexandra." Manrepeller.com. https://www.manrepeller.com/2019/09/the-cult-of-susan-alexandra.html. (accessed January 26, 2020).

Susan's fan base runs the gamut from the fashion-obsessed to the angsty teenager, both demographics known for being among the most active users on Instagram. Understanding this, and knowing that her core audience most likely found her on Instagram to begin with (thanks to the viral nature of her posts and celebrities from Gigi Hadid to Suri Cruise rocking her beaded bags all over the platform), Susan finds ways to perpetually capture their interest while simultaneously growing her brand. For example, Susan invited all of her Instagram fans to tune into her Bat Mitzvah via social media.

While almost all fashion houses connect to their core audiences on Instagram, few can say their followers are as highly engaged and loyal as Susan's. So, for Fashion Week, Susan greeted her fans exactly where she knew they would be—on Instagram—and gifted them the ultimate juxtaposition to trite fashion content: a uniquely Instagram-friendly Bat Mitzvah.

COPYCATS

A known downside of broadcasting any creative venture like Susan's so publicly is the fact that everyone else is going to try and replicate your magic. Susan has had to deal with well-known fashion retailers knocking off her beaded designs and selling them in big box stores on Fifth Avenue. She notes the knock-off world "is definitely one of the hardest things about being a creative on Instagram," and that implementing a strategy to curb copycats has been one of her biggest business challenges to date.

Regardless, Susan is unwilling to alter her Instagram presence or the way she connects with her loyal fan base, knowing that copycats are always lurking, no matter what medium she chooses to use. Manufacturing cheap knockoffs of Susan's designs is one thing, but being able to capture the *je ne sais quoi* of Susan's appeal is quite another. While they say imitation is the sincerest form of flattery, you cannot simply recreate Susan's magic, regardless of how big your budget is or how many prime retail locations you have across the world.

Would I be surprised to see a competitor's Bat Mitzvah marketing exhibition on the fashion calendar in the coming months? In this day and age, not really. But I can say with absolute certainty that it will never make the impact that Susan's original party did.

FLOYD HOME

You can try out a sofa in a furniture showroom, but that's not indicative of how it will look in your own home. As an alternative, many furniture companies offer digital options enabling you to superimpose their furniture on 3D renderings of your own home. Still, it never really feels like the real thing until you buy the piece, get it to your house, move everything around, and take a long look.

To combat this, Floyd Home fully outfits pre-existing, popular Airbnbs in their furniture so you can see it, feel it, and live it before you buy it.

Floyd Home designs furniture for people who move often, namely millennials. According to Floyd, on average, millennials tend to stay in an apartment for nine to twelve months at a time before they move again.[34] Floyd founders Alex O'Dell and Kyle Hoff wanted to craft furniture that fits right into this lifestyle, as the previous options were big, bulky styles that are difficult to move without help (à la Restoration Hardware), or cheaply made minimalistic pieces that are not strong enough to withstand multiple moves (think: Ikea). Kyle explains, "We both felt that the furniture industry as a whole had failed to adapt to the changing needs of people living in cities ... We take what are traditionally cumbersome pieces of furniture and make them lasting, adaptable, and most importantly, easily shippable."[35]

The company started out with a single product, a set of table legs that are easy to affix underneath the surface of your choice, instantly turning that surface, like a piece of raw-edge wood or a sheet of vintage scrap metal, into a table on the spot. You can remove the legs just as easily, pack it up, unpack it later, and start over. Due to the overwhelming popularity of their original leg set, Floyd has since expanded to full tables, side tables, beds, bookshelves,

---

34 Scheffler, Daniel. "Detroit Upstart Floyd Wants to Change How We Furnish Our Homes." Curbed.com. https://www.curbed.com/2016/7/19/12197656/floyd-detroit-furniture-modular-diy. (accessed January 26, 2020).

35 Scheffler, Daniel. "Detroit Upstart Floyd Wants to Change How We Furnish Our Homes." Curbed.com. https://www.curbed.com/2016/7/19/12197656/floyd-detroit-furniture-modular-diy. (accessed January 26, 2020).

and more—all easy to build and take apart on a whim as your lifestyle necessitates.

Floyd also features great design principles, hitting another fixture of millennial life. Each piece boasts a sleek, Scandinavian-inspired aesthetic that fits seamlessly into the millennial creed. Combining esteemed design elements, high quality, and effortless mobility, Floyd furniture is the millennial dream.

UNDERSTANDING THE MARKET

When it comes to any marketing initiative, the first step is understanding where your audience is. The obvious place to reach Floyd's target consumer is Instagram, as over 64 percent of millennials in the United States use Instagram every single day.[36] But every brand trying to target the millennial demographic can say its core audience is on Instagram, right?

So, where *else* is Floyd's target consumer–the person who values city living, great design, and high-quality furniture? Perhaps this consumer type also values spending their money on experiences rather than things. Perhaps they also love to travel and experience other cultures the way they are meant to be experienced, as a local instead of as a tourist. Perhaps they would much rather be a guest in someone's home instead of aimlessly racking up hotel points. Perhaps they're constantly

36 Chen, Jenn. "Important Instagram Stats You Need to Know For 2020." Sproutsocial.com. https://sproutsocial.com/insights/instagram-stats/. (accessed January 26, 2020).

looking for the perfect weekend getaway. This person is most certainly on Airbnb.

In addition to Instagram ads, Floyd set out to furnish some of its favorite Airbnbs in Los Angeles, Oregon, Montauk, The Catskills, Portland, San Francisco, and more. This allowed Floyd to reach its core demographic and offer prospective customers a way to live with Floyd furniture in a manner that resonated with their lifestyle, the way the furniture is meant to be lived in. All of this was done with the goal that maybe, just maybe, that millennial consumer will be inspired to buy some furniture for themselves.

In an *Architectural Digest* article profiling Floyd's strategic marketing move, Hadley Keller explains, "It's not such a far-fetched idea: As Airbnb has risen in popularity and become a haven for aesthetically-minded travelers looking for unique lodgings, it's become as much a source for design inspiration as vacation crashing."[37]

The brilliance of this marketing initiative is three-fold. First, it solves a problem unique to the furniture industry by giving prospective buyers the opportunity to "test drive" the products before buying them. Additionally, it enables Floyd to engage with its core demographic on Airbnb, a company whose business model naturally aligns itself with the values and lifestyle choices of Floyd's customers. Most importantly, this marketing

---

37 Keller, Hadley. "A New Way to Discover Furniture? In Your Airbnb." Architecturaldigest.com. https://www.architecturaldigest.com/story/a-new-way-to-discover-furniture-in-your-airbnb.(accessed January 26, 2020).

ploy affords Floyd the ability to stand out in a less crowded marketplace–as Airbnb is less crowded than Instagram–and make a bigger impact on its target demographic.

TAKEAWAYS

Both Susan Alexandra and Floyd Home understand that marketing for the sake of marketing is useless. For a brand to market effectively, it must remain true to its company values and allocate its customer acquisition spend in a manner that rings true with the brand's DNA. Both Susan Alexandra and Floyd Home effectively fuse online and offline initiatives to enhance their overall value proposition from the consumer's perspective.

Susan Alexandra and Floyd Home showcased the ability to precisely locate their target consumers and give them exactly what they want, *where they want it.* Both initiatives were successful because they simultaneously crafted unique experiences that supplement their social media initiatives, add to their value proposition, and increase visibility.

THE BOTTOM LINE

Go where your customers are.

As a business owner, you should constantly be doing whatever it takes to find out exactly where your target consumers spend the majority of their time, and if you find that they are on Instagram like Susan's, great! However, recognize that your competitors also think their customers are on Instagram, so in order to convert these people into paying customers, your branding and marketing angles must be uniquely creative.

If you find that your customers are on Instagram, but also decidedly somewhere else, be willing to meet them on another platform, like Floyd did on Airbnb.

And, if you're going to shell out big money for an Instagram-optimized marketing campaign, event, or perhaps a religious coming-of-age ceremony, it absolutely must be in line with your brand's ethos. The campaign or event must echo who you are and what you're about so that it blends seamlessly into all other aspects of your business–from your products to your logo design to everything else.

CHAPTER 17

YOU'VE GOTTA HAVE A GIMMICK!

RECESS

"Instead of paying Instagram to run ads, we want to pay *you!*" This was the message heard loud and clear by Recess's fifty thousand Instagram followers, in addition to the company's entire mailing list.

In the middle of the holiday shopping rush, Recess, a CBD-infused seltzer brand, ran a daylong campaign on Black Friday offering to Venmo three dollars to every person who promoted the beverage on his or her Instagram story. The offer wasn't aimed at the Insta-famous set. It wasn't even targeting micro-influencers. Instead, the promotional offer was available to any and all fans of the beverage. If you were looking to become three dollars richer, all you had to do was submit a screenshot of your post proving that you promoted Recess on your Instagram story.

The Recess team is known for trying new, innovative methods to spread the word about the brand on Instagram, despite the platform's restrictions on CBD products as they relate to native advertising.

Recess's clever Venmo stunt was a brilliant way to sidestep Instagram's strict regulations without technically breaking any rules. Furthermore, Recess was able to tap into a larger audience than they could have otherwise.

"Everything we do at Recess is about generating earned media, word-of-mouth, and buzz," Recess's founder Benjamin Witte tells *Adweek*. "The whole marketing strategy of Recess has been to create content and experiences, both digital and physical, that our community wants to engage with deeply and share with their friends."[38]

Benjamin adds, "Even if I could do paid advertising on Instagram, I'd still suspect we'd do very little of it ... someone telling someone else about a product is a thousand times more valuable than a paid ad conveying the same information."

WORD OF MOUTH

Nothing gets people talking like a good gimmick. For brands, the ability to make the leap from marketing gimmick to conversation starter to new sales driver is the ultimate goal.

---

38 Hiebert, Paul. "This CBD Brand Found a Workaround to Instagram's Cannabis Promotion Rules." Adweek.com https://www.adweek.com/brand-marketing/this-cbd-brand-paid-people-3-via-venmo-to-promote-its-post/. (accessed January 26, 2020).

The merits of word-of-mouth advertising speak for themselves. According to a recent report from Deloitte on this very topic, "customers acquired through word of mouth or referral marketing have a 37% higher retention rate" than through other means.[39] For any brand, crafting a strategy that gets people talking is always going to be a worthy objective. Remember the Marketing Funnel from Chapter 6? Word-of-mouth advocacy is the final step of the funnel that starts the cycle over again, triggering the beginning of an entirely new funnel full of fresh, potential customers for the desirable cost of zero dollars.

Recess's astute Venmo play sure got people talking. The promotion quickly went viral and Recess ran through its budget for this particular campaign in under twenty-four hours. As an added bonus, the campaign caught the attention of the press and was covered by various media outlets in the beverage, CBD, and advertising industries.

What's even more noteworthy is the timing. The Venmo campaign was able to cut through the noise on Black Friday, when the competition to acquire new customers is at its annual peak. Similarly, it's the one day of the year when all brands can justify spending more on customer acquisition because, well, 'tis the season! The best metric by which to judge the effectiveness of a marketing campaign will always

---

39 Murphy, Brandon. "Harnessing the Power of Consumer Advocacy to Fuel Effective Growth." Deloitte. https://www.slideshare.net/brandonmurphy/brand-advocacy-and-social-media-2009-gma-conference. accessed January 26, 2020).

be sales generated. The success of Recess's campaign was made quite evident when orders through the brand's website skyrocketed to almost 600 percent more than the company's previous daily average.

Word-of-mouth buzz is the most valuable type of earned media a brand can strive for. In a time when we are conditioned to reluctantly accept online reviews at face value, personal recommendations carry more weight. Recess cracked this code, enabling members of its network to tap into *their* networks while simultaneously boosting awareness, credibility, and sales.

BARBARA CORCORAN

While working for Barbara Corcoran, the most valuable lesson I learned from her was that "The most effective way to build a brand is not by spending money on advertising, but by finding a clever way to keep your name in the press."

When pressed for more clarity, Barbara would always respond with the same business mantra:

"You've got to have a gimmick!"

Barbara Corcoran has said this on Shark Tank, she's said it in person, she's said it in press interviews. Barbara has said it so many times I could recite it in my sleep. This was a Barbara Corcoran signature line, and the message was one of my biggest takeaways from our time together.

Barb was famous for her use of gimmicks to sell real estate throughout her career. She was always finding new and innovative ways to get people talking and keep them talking, too. Ultimately, it was the sale of the real estate empire bearing her name that transformed her into the titan of industry we know her as today.

In the 1980s, Barb differentiated herself in the male-dominated real estate sector with clever gimmicks at every opportunity she had. The press ate up each and every one of them.

- One time, she hosted an open-to-the-public "smudge ceremony" to get rid of the bad vibes at one of the apartments she was attempting to sell.
- Another time, she staged a pet training class to prepare pets for their co-op board interviews.
- She even (ingeniously) published The Madonna Report, a hypothetical list of NYC apartments Madonna might have been interested in purchasing. However, Barb created the list without ever speaking to Madonna. Needless to say, The Madonna Report spread like wildfire and the "Madonna-ready" apartments sold just as fast!

Each of these creative stunts became the talk of the real estate industry while also gaining coverage in the mainstream press. This compounded exposure gave Barbara access to a larger pool of potential customers than she ever could have reached, had she chosen to stick with the tried and true, traditional methods of real estate advertising. Each stunt brought in new business and paved the way for Barbara Corcoran to become the household name she is today.

It goes without saying that the landscape for obtaining press coverage and executing innovative advertising strategies has shifted dramatically from where it was in the 1980s. However, the core principles remain the same. Brands must focus on inventive and original approaches to spread the word, differentiate themselves from the competition, and ultimately drive sales, with gimmicks as the perfect way to do it all.

GIMMICKS

Colloquially, the word "gimmick" often has cheap or even negative connotations. Yet, when properly executed, a marketing gimmick has quite the opposite effect on a brand's bottom line. A well-conceived gimmick, whether on Instagram, *Page Six*, or *The Wall Street Journal*, gets people talking and acts as a timeless and highly effective sales tool. Remember the infamous Dollar Shave Club video? How about the Geico Gecko or the Aflac Duck? Of course you do–that's my point. As Recess has proven, a well-executed gimmick will drive word-of-mouth advertising across platforms and get you closer to your customer's wallet.

Finally, as the Queen of Gimmicks, Barbara Corcoran, has demonstrated with her brilliant marketing tactics ... well, you know how those turned out! To understand the true value of a gimmick is to look beyond the conversational implications of the word itself and recognize that the commercial success it yields is anything but cheap.

CHAPTER 18

GOING WHOLESALE

MEGABABE

Katie Sturino loves summer. Her ideal day (and mine too, by the way) is spent in a bikini by the pool at a luxury resort in Italy, basking in the sun until dinner time, when she'll slip into a brightly colored caftan and dine under the Tuscan moon until it's time to go to bed and start the fun all over again.

It isn't always easy for Katie to make her endless summer dream a reality. Aside from the obvious geographical roadblocks (she lives in Manhattan), Katie has a skin condition that prohibits her from spending too much time in the sun. Worst of all, she suffers from unbearable thigh chafing that is exacerbated by the heat.

Katie made a name for herself on Instagram as an outspoken champion for plus-size women and by promoting inclusive sizing among fashion brands. Katie didn't care about the unspoken "rules" dictating what she could and could not share publicly on Instagram, so she went full steam ahead, used her feed to rant about her thigh chafe (among other things), and amassed a loyal following of almost half a million women with common interests and shared experiences.

Katie's honesty was a breath of fresh air and cemented her status as one of Instagram's most prominent influencers. Given her significant and engaged following, Katie knew that if she started a consumer product company, it had a great chance of taking off.

Still searching for a solution to her problematic thigh chafe and brimming with confidence from the positive reinforcement of her followers, Katie founded Megababe. She began with a simple product designed for women who were sick of the discomfort caused by their legs rubbing together all day. Katie drained her savings to make the first batch of Thigh Rescue, her solution to thigh chafe, and prayed for the best.

Initially, it was all she could do, as Katie found it difficult to convince investors and beauty industry gatekeepers to buy into her vision. Many beauty industry executives were not willing to recognize Thigh Rescue as a women's essential because they had never heard of the thigh chafe problem before. They didn't realize they had never heard of the problem because women are often too embarrassed to discuss chafing publicly. The subject was particularly taboo in fashion circles.

However, Katie has a knack for speaking her mind, defying social norms, and redefining what's cool. Thus, ridding the world of thigh chafe became the perfect problem for her to solve. Katie applied the same say-anything, no-holds-barred approach she takes in her everyday life to promoting her company, preaching to her followers about a new solution to their summer chafing woes.

Based on initial feedback from Instagram, Katie knew Megababe had the potential to be big–mega big. Yet, as a founder, she was in a difficult position.

GOING WHOLESALE

Katie knew that in order to recoup her initial investment and grow her business, tapping into her followers and betting on a strictly direct-to-consumer play would not be enough. Megababe would need to explore wholesale opportunities. Despite how much Katie wanted wholesale accounts, industry gatekeepers were not initially interested in taking on a new brand that was solving a problem they did not know existed or barely understood. Reluctantly, Katie forged ahead as a strictly direct-to-consumer, e-commerce brand, marketing exclusively on Instagram while always keeping wholesale in the back of her mind. On the heels of a successful launch, Katie's first run of Thigh Rescue sold out immediately and Megababe amassed a thirteen-thousand-person waitlist for her next batch.

Is a thirteen-thousand-person waitlist enough to land a wholesale account? It turns out when coupled with loyal fans, a great press strategy and an even better product, the answer is a resounding *yes.*

Katie elaborates: "I knew no matter what we needed wholesale and for me, I personally needed Target. I love Target and I knew my product needed to be at Target. But Target is *Target* so it wasn't, you know, the easiest thing, but we *are* in Target. And being in Target is a status symbol for any brand that will allow us to do bigger things in the future."

HITTING THE BULLSEYE

Target is the holy grail of big box retail. Landing an account with Target comes with cache and can legitimize a brand overnight. For entrepreneurs, selling products through Target is more of a status symbol than being verified on Instagram. At the same time, being in Target opens a brand up to a whole host of new customers the brand may not have been able to reach before.

As discussed in Chapter 3, The Direct-To-Consumer Landscape, many new brands opt to forgo wholesale entirely in favor of selling directly to their consumers. The idea is that when a brand sells its product in bulk, the brand sells the wholesaler its product at half of the going retail price. When the product is on the shelf at the wholesale store, the wholesaler doubles the price it paid to stock the product so that the new sticker price is equal to the price the brand sells it for on its own. This way, both the brand and the wholesaler charge the same amount for a given product, so consumers pay the same price, whether they are purchasing the product directly from the brand or from a wholesale vendor.

Proponents of the direct-to-consumer model say they would rather sell an item at full price themselves than sell numerous items at half price, making the argument that it is cheaper for them to acquire customers directly (though platforms like Instagram) than to share a cut of their profits with a wholesaler in exchange for customer acquisition. However, when the rising costs of customer acquisition on platforms like Facebook and Instagram are factored in, the direct-to-consumer model loses its luster.

Katie recognized that building her business in the mold of a strictly direct-to-consumer brand with an online-only presence had the potential be a short-term, cost-effective strategy. However, she realized this business model was not a sustainable solution for the long haul. Katie knew that her followers could help her hit major sales milestones in the beginning, but in order to become profitable and to scale her business for multi-year growth, she needed wholesale. And as mentioned, on a personal level, she really wanted the prestige of being in the retail holy grail of Target.

In addition to the cache of "being in Target," Target's financials shed light on why beauty brands clamor to get in the door like single guys waiting in line outside of the hottest nightclub du jour.

In 2018, Target's revenue topped seventy-five billion dollars with the wholesaler's beauty lines comprising a whopping

24 percent of its gross revenue.[40] If Megababe could share in the upside of Target's eighteen-billion-dollar beauty line specific revenue stream, it would elevate the startup into another stratosphere of profitability. As an influencer-founded company, Megababe is set up for long-term success because Katie was willing to diversify the brand's customer touch points instead of relying solely on Instagram. At the end of the day, Katie hit the bullseye by landing the Target account, focusing on wholesale to propel her company toward mega profitability.

ADINA'S JEWELS

Adina Kamkhatchi founded her namesake jewelry line when she was eighteen years old. As if this weren't impressive enough, she has managed to turn her brand into a cult favorite, with pieces worn by celebrities from Billie Eilish to Cardi B to Emily Ratajkowski. What's more? She's built Adina's Jewels into a multimillion-dollar business in just two years.

As a Gen-Z entrepreneur, it was only fitting that Adina started her business and initial marketing efforts on social media, Instagram specifically. In an effort to scale, Adina branched out and landed her first big retail partnership with Nordstrom. In tandem with Nordstrom, Adina's Jewels sells over 150 styles in the forty-to 150-dollar range, which is in line with

---

40 Smith, Craig. "45 Interesting Facts About Target." Expandedramblings.com. https://expandedramblings.com/index.php/target-statistics/. (accessed January 26, 2020).

Nordstrom's target price point and market segment. This year, Adina's Jewels landed another impressive account, partnering with upscale Neiman Marcus to sell its higher-end jewelry, pieces made from 14-karat gold and diamonds, fetching up to $698 each.[41]

By expanding into both lower and higher-end wholesale doors, Adina's Jewels now has access to two new markets and benefits from being exposed to shoppers in both. Department store shoppers who are unfamiliar with Adina's Jewels but learn about the brand while seeing it displayed in Nordstrom or Neiman Marcus inherently trust that if verified brands like Nordstrom and Neiman Marcus carry the line, it must be legit.

As a result, brands that take the wholesale approach learn firsthand that the wholesale seal of approval often lowers customer acquisition costs significantly, negating the cut wholesalers take when buying from brands at the standard reduced rate.

NEW AVENUES

While brands are recognizing the benefits of getting their product on wholesale shelves, a new crop of businesses are creating innovative avenues to help formerly digitally-native companies make their way into physical locations for the first time.

---

41 Richards, Katie. "Built on Instagram, Adina's Jewels is looking to department stores for new customers." Glossy.com. https://www.glossy.co/fashion/built-on-instagram-adinas-jewels-is-looking-to-department-stores-for-new-customers. (accessed January 26, 2020).

Bulletin, a New York City based startup with three retail locations, recognized the difficulties of small brands getting wholesale accounts, like mandatory attendance at prohibitively expensive trade shows and attempting to cut fair deals with predatory wholesale representatives. As a hassle-free alternative, Bulletin "pioneered an innovative co-retailing model that [has] helped hundreds of brands access affordable, premium retail space across New York City."[42] Acting as a curator, Bulletin hand-selects unique products to showcase in its own store locations. Instead of Bulletin taking a typical wholesale cut of 50 percent off the retail price, brands pay a monthly fee to secure their shelf space and let Bulletin handle the rest.

With more demand than physical space, Bulletin launched a digital platform that connects its vetted brands with other wholesale vendors across the world. By directly leasing shelf space or connecting brands with wholesalers, Bulletin offers brands all the benefits of wholesale with none of the headaches.

Similarly, Showfields, the self-proclaimed "most interesting store in the world," has reimagined the department store model with its four-story retail concept in Manhattan. Direct-to-consumer brands looking to experiment with a physical sales presence can also lease space from Showfields. In turn, Showfields promotes the brand and drives foot traffic towards the space by way of events and special programming.

---

42 "Bulletin FAQ," Bulletin Brands. https://bulletin.co/faq/meet-bulletin. (accessed January 26, 2020).

Showfields' concept is a hybrid wholesale-retail model, as brands can build out their section of the store however they want and make it their own while remaining part of a larger, hyper-curated department store scene.

Both Bulletin and Showfields are able to carve out space in the wholesale world for a better way of doing business as the direct-to-consumer landscape shifts increasingly offline.

LEVERAGE

As direct-to-consumer brands begin to realize the difficulty of acquiring customers on their own, the benefits of selling to wholesale accounts look increasingly more appealing.

Hilary Milnes, a reporter for *Digiday*, elaborates on this growing trend. "Online brands like Harry's, Casper, Native, Quip, The Arrivals, Alala, Bark, and Reformation have started selling in wholesale retailers like Target, Nordstrom and Shopbop, as digital growth has proven to be limiting and standalone physical stores are difficult to scale. It turns out that the middlemen that many of these formerly direct-to-consumer brands tried to remove from the retail equation still have a reason for existing."[43]

From a brand's perspective, the primary benefit of wholesale has not changed. Partnering with a wholesaler allows brands

---

43 Milnes, Hilary. "A Giant Billboard for the Company': How Digitally Native Brands are Navigating Wholesale Partnerships." Digiday.com. https://digiday.com/marketing/giant-billboard-company-digitally-native-brands-negotiate-wholesale-partnerships/. (accessed January 26, 2020).

the opportunity to reach sizable swaths of customers who were previously inaccessible. Wholesalers used to have all the power when it came to selecting new brands to include in their stores.

This is no longer the case today, however, as direct-to-consumer brands are able to enter into wholesale agreements with more leverage than ever before. Why? Because today's brands come armed with vast amounts of data on their customers that wholesalers have not had access to in the past. And, to anyone trying to sell in today's landscape, specific consumer data equals power.

Tricia Smith, former Executive Vice President of Nordstrom's Women's Apparel, speaks to the change in trends from the wholesale perspective. "[Nordstrom's] used to be transactional, and now we have a higher degree of transparency and collaboration [with new brands]. We have to be open. We can't say, 'This is how you'll work with us,' not if we want their business."[44]

The sun appears to be setting on the days of wholesalers bullying brands into submission with inflexible negotiation points and unfair term sheets. This has given rise to a new dawn in which direct-to-consumer brands, armed with mountains of invaluable consumer data often sourced

44 Milnes, Hilary. "How Nordstrom Changed its Merchandising Strategy for the DTC Brand Era." Glossy.co. https://www.glossy.co/fashion/how-nordstrom-changed-its-merchandising-strategy-for-the-dtc-brand-era. (accessed January 26, 2020).

from Instagram and Facebook, are the new power brokers in today's wholesale agreements.

BY ROBYNBLAIR

In an effort to stay relevant, traditional wholesalers are opening their doors to younger, smaller brands much earlier than they have in the past. The latest Instagram darling to make a major splash in wholesale is Robyn Davidson, whose brand, By Robynblair, serves as the perfect example of this remarkable commercial shift.

In 2018, By Robynblair took the creative, fashion, and Instagram worlds by storm when Robyn started offering fine art in the form of Lucite-encased candy with catchy phrases like "In Case of Emergency Break Glass" splashed across the front. Each piece is bright, colorful, and sassy, enabling her unique designs to serve as the ideal Instagram posts every single time. Influencers, celebrities, and everyday fans (like moi!) rushed to get their hands on custom By Robynblair artwork. Robyn capitalized on her tidal wave of success by releasing more affordable brand extensions, like candy dishes, in her signature style.

Other brands were also quick to take note of Robyn's success and clamored to partner with her in co-branded collaborations. Examples of Robyn's hit collaborations include a partnership with trendy phone case brand Off My Case, which produced a custom run of candy-inspired, protective cases, a deal with Insta-famous jeweler Stephanie Gottlieb, which led to a line of bespoke candy-inspired jewelry and jewelry boxes, and a relationship with home décor e-tailer Dormify, which produced an affordable print line of Robyn's signature styles, to name a few.

Co-branded collaborations are an easy way for brands to keep their current client base happy with new product releases while getting double exposure to the partner brand's network of customers. These types of collaborations are a mutually beneficial byproduct of the direct-to-consumer era where brands can rely on other brands for an extra boost in awareness, exposure, and sales–previously a role only an established wholesaler could fill.

As wholesalers begin to recognize they are on the short end of this shift in power dynamics, they are scrambling to adapt and keep pace. Recently, Bergdorf Goodman, arguably the most esteemed department store in New York City, reached out to collaborate with Robyn, recognizing that a partnership with her includes access to loyal, hyper-engaged fans who will rush to support her latest and greatest endeavor. As such, Robyn's foray into traditional wholesale includes an entire seventh floor takeover at one of the most prestigious wholesalers in the world. The floor features various rooms full of Robyn's work, all in a picture-perfect, Insta-friendly fashion that offers multiple backdrops for content creation and, of course, geo-tagging!

The vignettes (think: a rainbow room, a neon cloud dreamscape, a life-size ice cream truck) are inherently postable, designed specifically for the social media era and are ripe for fans of both Bergdorf Goodman and By Robynblair to share with their own networks.

Of course, Bergdorf Goodman customers can purchase any of Robyn's offerings right off the store wall. However, instead of the historical wholesale agreement where Bergdorf Goodman would insist on taking fifty percent of the retail price, Robyn was able to leverage the current direct-to-consumer landscape while negotiating a more favorable deal and still cashing in on the added exposure from her takeover.

Though Bergdorf Goodman can boast that it is now the premier retail destination for one of the most popular names in art and fashion, the real winner is Robyn. By Robynblair products are proudly displayed and sold at Bergdorf Goodman without the strong-arming and unfair revenue split that might have plagued a young brand's relationship with the department store only a few years ago. Why? Because at this stage in the wholesale landscape, Bergdorf Goodman needs brands like By Robynblair more than brands like By Robynblair need Bergdorf Goodman.

The road back to wholesale has opened up new, creative paths for digitally native brands to get their product in front of customers' faces without the previous negative side effects. At the same time, legacy wholesalers and department stores are scrambling to keep up, making the process more transparent than ever so that new brands can move in and explore the wholesale route, in search of new customers.

CHAPTER 19

THE ROAD TO RETAIL

LALO

Soon-to-be dad Greg Davidson took a poll.

He asked his friends who, like him at the time, did not have kids of their own, which brands they most associate with the word "baby." The usual suspects, like Johnson & Johnson, Gerber, and Pampers were all thrown around as the quintessential brands of the baby world.

However, when Greg asked the same question to his friends who were already parents, their answers were completely different.

He found a substantial disconnect between the brands non-parents associate with the word "baby" and the brands parents actually rely on to care for their children. Greg quickly learned what all soon-to-be-parents also come to realize: navigating the baby world, especially as a first-time parent, is really, really confusing. So, he founded Lalo, a cute abbreviation for "Love All Little Ones," to cut through the confusion.

Lalo's hero product is a stroller meant for daily use, but Lalo isn't just in the business of making consumer goods. Lalo's principal mission is to help first-time parents debunk the myths, misconceptions, and confusion evident in all aspects of early parenthood. If the brand's expert guidance persuades a new parent to purchase one of its products, it's a win-win.

BUILDING TRUST

Depending on the consumer category you are in, brand trust matters in varying degrees.

Buying a new parachute? Brand trust matters a *lot*. You need to be sure that you're buying from a brand that you trust is up to date on all safety measures and compliances, which is why you're most likely not going to purchase a parachute from a company you've never heard of before.

Buying a new tank top? A loose stitch in the tank top's seam is likely not going to kill you, (whereas a loose stitch in the parachute's seam almost certainly will). The likelihood of you buying a tank top from a company you've never heard of before is much higher than that of a parachute.

Parachutes aside, one consumer category is in a league of its own when it comes to requiring the highest amount of perceived trust amongst its consumers: the baby category. For new brands attempting to break into this highly competitive and established industry, earning consumers' trust is not just something to work towards, but rather an immediate requisite for survival. There is absolutely zero margin for error and the headline risk simply cannot be overstated.

Given that Lalo was a brand-new company, Greg realized that his first order of business had to be establishing trust with new customers. Traditionally, baby companies used fear-mongering tactics to persuade parents to buy their products, preying on the fact parents would do anything to ensure their baby's safety. While safety is of course one of Lalo's core values, the brand refused to scare customers into purchasing products. Instead, Lalo focused on cultivating a loyal, caring community that would inherently trust that safety was built into everything Lalo does.

As a direct-to-consumer brand in the digital world, Lalo launched on all social media platforms. However, Greg quickly realized it was impossible to earn the necessary magnitude of consumer trust through a screen, especially when a brand is starting from scratch. With regard to Lalo's initial social media advertising strategy, Greg explains, "We weren't building trust–we were just trying to drive conversion. We knew we needed to find other meaningful ways to drive trust to get a much more valuable customer."

At this point in the pay-to-play digital ad landscape, the company with the most money to spend is most likely to get the sale because they can afford to target, and retarget ... and retarget you again, dear customer, until you buy. Yet, ad spend and precise targeting are meaningless for a fledgling baby company if customers do not trust the brand from the start.

Realizing the company's Facebook and Instagram strategy was not yielding the consumer trust necessary for the brand to grow and succeed, Greg decided to explore other strategies to help Lalo reach its goals.

GOING RETAIL

Greg found that when you build trust offline, it's easier to drive conversions online.

In order to demonstrate the brand's dependability to potential customers, the Lalo team decided to let customers join them in the office ... literally. Enter The Lalo Loft, a hybrid office-showroom-store in New York City where prospective customers can come in and take strollers for a test-drive, examine products in person, and (most importantly) interact with Greg and his team.

Want to see if your baby will be comfy in his or her new ride? Pop your little one right in! Potential buyers are treated "like family," which is exactly the point, not just an Olive Garden catchphrase.

Creating a family-friendly environment helps Lalo establish necessary and highly-coveted brand trust, giving the business a leg up on its uniquely competitive industry.

Once you buy into the Lalo lifestyle, you are invited to return with your baby for kid-centric programming like music class and playgroup where you can meet like-minded parents navigating the baby world for the first time just like you. And, after class, if you find yourself in need of a highchair, Lalo has one you can try out at the Loft and bring home that night.

Greg and Lalo's story highlights the importance of building trust and cultivating a community while building your brand, with physical retail serving as the connective tissue between your business and consumer. Retail and trust go hand in hand, especially in the most delicate industries, and Lalo's bottom line proves that investing in physical space works far better than relying on digital ads and clicks.

Lalo's emphasis on offline community building demonstrates how much higher the value of your customer is when they trust you versus when they have merely heard of you from an Instagram ad. These Lalo converts are every brand's dream. Not only will they become repeat customers, but they are also more likely to tell their newly expecting friends to stop by your store.

THE NEW RETAIL LANDSCAPE

Even the staunchest initial supporters of the digitally native direct-to-consumer model have been changing their tune when it comes to retail locations. Think Warby Parker, Glossier, Away, Bonobos, Everlane, and more. A lot more.

The biggest takeaway from our current retail landscape is not that these formerly online-only efforts have failed, but that their online efforts only got them so far. These brands simply outgrew the model they created. As such, retail is the logical next step for brands looking to take their digital business to the next level.

Increasingly, digitally-native brands with robust social media presences are expanding into physical brick-and-mortar locations to lower customer acquisition costs, tell their stories, communicate with their customers, and gain real-time feedback from real time clients. Here are some examples:

- Understanding the value of both online and offline consumer data, La Ligne, an apparel line of easy, effortless stripes and solids, opened its first store to capitalize on both. Co-Founder Molly Howard elaborates to *Vogue*, "The great thing about being direct-to-consumer is that you have so much data on your customer—who she is, where she lives, what she buys ... You really get to know them, but it's still behind a screen. It's great to get feedback in an email, but it's different hearing it in person. That's the gift of having this physical space."[45] Certain data points cannot be easily communicated through a screen. For example, how is your customer dressed? Is she shopping alone or with friends? Is she looking for a specific item or just browsing? Best of all, with a physical retail space, you have the opportunity to establish a friendly rapport with your customers. When given a choice, people would always rather do business with their friends!

---

45 Fara, Emily. "La Ligne's First Store is Opening Today on Madison Avenue." Vogue.com. https://www.vogue.com/article/la-ligne-first-store-new-york. (accessed January 26, 2020).

- Having a physical connection to your living space is a core tenant of lifestyle brand Hill House, so forgoing the brick-and-mortar route was a non-starter. Founder Nell Diamond explains her desire to branch out into retail stems from the fact that it is the best way for the digitally native brand to tell the Hill House story the Hill House way. Nell explains, "I've always been obsessed with the stories brands tell through products and experiences, and there is no better place to tell these stories than in person. I was desperate to find a home base for Hill House that allowed us to tell our own story, and allowed customers to walk into the world we've created ... Having a physical space to speak to customers, share our story, and merchandise our product has been a dream for me."[46] Nell's emphasis on in-person storytelling resonated with her shoppers, as the Hill House team has now outgrown its original Bleecker Street store and is expanding into a larger space later this year.

- Lingua Franca sweaters are natural conversation starters. Each piece features a hand-embroidered, witty, often political, saying front and center. Founder Rachelle Hruska MacPherson speaks to her company's desire for a physical space that is in line with her brand's offerings, telling *Town and Country Magazine* that when it came to opening Lingua Franca's first store downtown, "It's not

---

46 Arsenault, Bridget. "Inside Hill House Home: A New Female-Founded Brand Shaking Up the Retail Industry." Forbes.com. https://www.forbes.com/sites/bridgetarsenault/2019/11/18/inside-hill-house-home-a-new-female-founded-brand-shaking-up-the-retail-industry/#27ed26085b77. (accessed January 26, 2020).

> about selling sweaters. It's about starting conversations."[47] Starting conversations in person is the only logical step for a brand whose most popular offering is a conversation-starting sweater. Riding the success of its first store downtown, Lingua Franca's second retail space opened last year on Madison Avenue, bringing its banter uptown.

La Ligne, Hill House, and Lingua Franca are all Insta-darling companies with sizable followings that recognize the inherent value of in-person connections in tandem with their respective online presences. Each has raced to build out stores of its own to accommodate growing demand, learn firsthand about its clientele, and spur its bottom line.

BRICK AND MORTAR OF THE FUTURE

The most glaring roadblocks to traditional retail are the costs associated with opening a physical location from scratch. These costs include (but are not limited to) broker fees, legal fees, store build outs, interior and exterior design, construction, hiring and training talent, inventory management, and, last but not least, rent. It goes without saying that opening a brick-and-mortar location is a costly and daunting proposition for new brands.

However, new companies are serving as the bridge between digitally native brands and the retail locations necessary to scale their businesses. Leap, a retail infrastructure startup,

---

47 Cantrell, Liz. "Lingua Franca Opens its First Retail Store." Townandcountrymag.com. https://www.townandcountrymag.com/style/fashion-trends/a25008888/lingua-franca-first-retail-store-new-york-city/. (accessed January 26, 2020).

handles the costly and overwhelming, logistical legwork for digitally native brands looking to take the "leap" by expanding into brick and mortar retail. Leap takes care of leasing, staffing, store design, and data integration, which allows founders to seamlessly transition their businesses into new retail locations without taking time away from critical sales opportunities. Leap's CEO, Amish Tolia elaborates: "The right brands want to focus on brand building, great product innovation, new collections, scaling supply chain and marketing. They don't want to get bogged down by the details of what it takes to execute a great retail strategy. Leap is a platform they can use to build and operate stores at scale."[48]

On behalf of startups across the country, Leap provides infrastructure solutions to many of the challenges brands face when expanding into retail for the first time. The company's unique value proposition has encouraged many digitally native businesses to take advantage of the plentiful and lucrative sales opportunities that live offline.

CURRENT REAL ESTATE ADVISORS

Another company helping brands ease into retail is Current Real Estate Advisors, a commercial real estate firm bridging the gap between social media and commercial real estate. Partners Brandon Charnas and Adam Henick realized there was more to real estate than legal jargon and lease execution, and their business has exploded because of it.

48 Richards, Katie. "How Naadam is Subtracting Risk From its Physical Retail Expansion." Glossy.co. https://www.glossy.co/fashion/how-naadam-is-subtracting-risk-from-its-physical-retail-expansion. (accessed January 26, 2020).

When digitally-native businesses partner with Current to source their first retail location, they receive far more than a simple segue into a store front in return. Current also works on behalf of its clients to drive traffic to their new retail locations. Simply put, Current doesn't just help you get your store–Current helps you get people *into* your store. This additional value proposition underscores why Current prides itself on a business model that is far more expansive than that of traditional commercial real-estate brokerages. Additionally, no better brokerage exists to transition digitally native businesses into retail, because no one understands the synergies between social media and real estate better than Brandon and Adam.

BRIDGING RETAIL AND SOCIAL

Current Real Estate has access to thousands of shoppers through its own network channels. It's a significant differentiator when co-founder Brandon Charnas, who is married to lifestyle influencer Arielle Charnas of Something Navy, is able to leverage a social media presence of over 1.6 million followers on behalf of Current's real estate clients. Brandon explains, "Social media presented the leasing platform as a scalable business. It allows us to branch out and provide [our clients] another service that doesn't cost us anything. At the same time, we're getting more and more clients, and our clients are getting more and more customers."

When opening a new store, most retailers worry that it will not attract enough customers to justify the significant rental expenditure. Current's clients are able to erase that fear and replace it with the question of "will we be able to handle the sheer volume of shoppers visiting our store after Current's network posts about our opening?". Current actively promotes its tenant's spaces, ensuring a strong customer presence from day one.

Brandon and Adam realized early on that the success of their business and tenants was not mutually exclusive. As such, they have taken advantage of a brokerage model that enables them to naturally align Current's incentives with those of its tenants. In other words, Current thrives when its tenants thrive, as both parties benefit from the added exposure and increase in sales. If Current can drive enough shoppers to a client's first retail location, it will most likely be retained to handle the client's second, third, and fourth locations as well.

As the digital landscape has proven, all aspects of business, from lease agreements to social media, are intertwined, and today's industry leaders are those who are quick to capitalize on the opportunity this connectivity provides. While brands race to open their own store locations, working with firms like Leap and Current Real Estate Advisors help ease the pain points retail has historically presented.

Interestingly, the "retail-pocalypse" phenomenon, the idea that traditional retail is dead, which has only been reinforced by the stream of legacy brands closing up shop, makes this an ideal time for new startups to move in. In fact, it's never been easier for brands to make the jump into retail. Showrooms, pop-up locations, and excess ground floor inventory are all viable options in this new, anything-goes landscape that is a product of legacy brands dying out.

When a company has a finite amount of money to spend on its next big customer acquisition push, it will commonly weigh its options between going the brick and mortar route and upping its digital advertising spend. At a glance, it's easy to write off brick and mortar as too expensive, given the majority of the costs occur up front. Conversely, with social media ad spend, brands can choose to allocate the budget across a longer time frame that makes more sense from a fiscal perspective.

That said, to forgo the retail route in lieu of a social media advertising play is a short-sighted approach when new companies offer viable solutions to this unique commercial challenge.

CONCLUSION

ASHLEY LONGSHORE

Artist Ashley Longshore is a bona-fide hustler, and it shows. Describing her uncanny ability to sell her thirty-thousand-dollar punchy artwork straight off of Instagram, Ashley tells *Vogue*, "I can post a painting and it will sell before the paint is dry."[49]

By all accounts, Ashley, in her glitzy, over-the-top brazen manner, is an Instagram success story. She boasts over 250 thousand hyper-engaged, die-hard fans who eat up everything she says and designs. Yet, Ashley would be the first to tell you that she does not attribute her Instagram popularity to the platform itself.

"Instagram is just a great way to stay connected to people [who] are interested in your work. That being said, social media and

---

49 Fleming, Olivia. "Why the World's Most Talked About Art Dealer is Instagram." Vogue.com. https://www.vogue.com/article/buying-and-selling-art-on-instagram. (accessed January 26, 2020).

Instagram are not the answer. You know, I spend so much of my time traveling to shows in other cities, marketing myself, and meeting people, and Instagram is the cherry on top–it isn't the spotlight!"

Ashley's success comes from week-long stretches of fourteen-hour days and good, old-fashioned hard work. Ashley's hard work manifests in many forms. She has taken part in a Gucci advertising campaign, designed a line of cosmetics with Maybelline, built a longstanding takeover of the Bergdorf Goodman Cafe in New York City, and written two books–*Ashley Longshore: I Do Not Cook, I Do Not Clean, I Do Not Fly Commercial* and *You Don't Look Fat, You Look Crazy: An Unapologetic Guide to Being Ambitchous*–all while operating her full-time art gallery in New Orleans. Clearly, Ashley has turned the notion of specialization on its head. She specializes in everything she touches. Her personality is her most valuable IP. Thankfully, her audacious and fun-loving persona is palpable in all of her creative endeavors.

During our conversation, Ashley elaborates that "There's a lot of inertia there that builds interest and that draws people to [my] Instagram account, other than just the Instagram account itself." Despite her unbridled success on the platform, Ashley also becomes frustrated with the misplaced hype that touts Instagram as a "one-stop shop" for cheap reach, sales, and profitability. "You just can't depend on one platform ... I mean, if we could figure out the algorithm and what makes consumers tick, then I'd be flying around on that new G7 right now, with diamonds hanging down in my vagina, but that just isn't the case!"

While Instagram helps spread the word about Ashley's art, it's her hustle, innate charisma, and natural talent that truly drive her success on and offline.

THE WORD "STARTUP"

While researching and interviewing entrepreneurs for this book, the word "startup" began to irritate me.

I started to notice that the word was carelessly thrown around to describe everything from glorified hobbies to billion-dollar brands like Glossier and Warby Parker. This got me thinking: what does it mean to be a *startup*? What separates a startup from a traditional *business*? When does a brand transition from a startup to an established *company*? While this modern word has a dictionary definition, what has it actually come to mean when we use it so frequently and casually to describe an enormous range of companies?

Before the word *startup* entered our lexicon, if you had an idea, were selling something, or building out your dreams, even in its earliest years you didn't have a startup–you had a *business*. The repetitive motion of ideating and selling, rinse and repeat, day in and day out was your life and livelihood, and you treated it as such.

As I dug deeper, I found the proliferation of the word startup coincided with the digitally native direct-to-consumer boom, and often, the word is used interchangeably by reporters, headlines and regular people as a lazy synonym for a digitally-native business.

This finding is not revolutionary by any means. However, I feel the overuse of the word "startup" cheapens the amount of work today's entrepreneurs must put into their businesses to be successful. The arbitrary way we use the word "startup" minimizes the sleepless nights and necessary bootstrapped problem solving, while replacing them with a veneer of shiny beer taps in the office kitchen and heated ping pong competitions in the staff room. Somehow, we've managed to psychologically trade in elbow grease for communal kombucha.

Additionally, it adds to the false narrative that starting a company is *easy*. What makes startup life seem so easy? The popular misconception that Instagram ads are a new company's cheap ticket to the promised land.

I would hope by now you recognize that this is not the case. Instagram ads alone are not the solution or cure for a business' sales woes.

In many of the case studies I profiled for this book, Instagram–whether it be organic posts or a robust advertising strategy–was a large part of the equation, or even the *desired* solution.

Yet, Instagram alone is not the reason any of these businesses reached their million- or billion-dollar valuations, no matter how much the Iceberg Illusion insists that it is.

APPENDIX

INTRODUCTION

1. Molla, Rani. Wagner, Kurt. "People Spend Almost as Much Time on Instagram as They Do on Facebook." Vox.com. https://www.vox.com/2018/6/25/17501224/instagram-facebook-snapchat-time-spent-growth-data. (accessed January 26, 2020).

THE ICEBERG THEORY

2. "Wikipedia: Iceberg Theory," Wikimedia Foundation, last modified December 18, 2019, 09:25, https://en.wikipedia.org/wiki/Iceberg_theory.

THE DIRECT-TO-CONSUMER LANDSCAPE

3. Swanson, Ana. "Meet the Four-Eyed, Eight-Tentacled Monopoly That is Making Your Glasses So Expensive.' Forbes.com https://www.forbes.com/sites/anaswanson/2014/09/10/meet-the-four-eyed-eight-tentacled-monopoly-that-is-making-your-glasses-so-expensive/#765283746b66 (January 26, 2020)

4. Swanson, Ana. "Meet the Four-Eyed, Eight-Tentacled Monopoly That is Making Your Glasses So Expensive.' Forbes.com https://www.forbes.com/sites/anaswanson/2014/09/10/meet-the-four-eyed-eight-tentacled-monopoly-that-is-making-your-glasses-so-expensive/#765283746b66 (January 26, 2020)

5. Warby Parker utilized a robust multi-pronged PR and marketing strategy, but the success of the direct-to-consumer model that they pioneered led many brands to want to keep cutting out more seemingly superfluous players from the equation, like PR and marketing.

HOW WE GOT HERE

6. Instagram. "Stand Out with Instagram." Instagram.com. https://business.instagram.com/getting-started/ (accessed January 26, 2020).

THE PERFECT STORM

7. Davis, Grant. "How One Woman's Cosmetic Company 'Gramed its Way to Insta-Success." Entrepreneur.com. https://www.entrepreneur.com/article/249328 (accessed January 26, 2020).

8. Fast Company. "Most Innovative Companies." Fastcompany.com. https://www.fastcompany.com/company/glossier. (accessed January 26, 2020).

INSTAGRAM ADS

9. Hodgson, Camilla. "How Start-Ups Have Used Instagram to Build $1Bn Businesses." Ft.com. https://www.ft.com/content/a5e69d68-4c36-11e9-bbc9-6917dce3dc62. (Accessed January 26, 2020).

10. Stanley, T.L. "Q&A: Dirty Lemon's Founder and Iris Nova CEO on the Future of the Drug Store." Adweek.com. https://www.adweek.com/brand-marketing/qa-dirty-lemons-founder-and-ceo-on-the-future-of-the-drug-store/. (Accessed January 26, 2020).

11. Hodgson, Camilla. "How Start-Ups Have Used Instagram to Build $1Bn Businesses." Ft.com. https://www.ft.com/content/a5e69d68-4c36-11e9-bbc9-6917dce3dc62. (Accessed January 26, 2020).

12. Liffreing, Ilyse. "Pivot to Traditional: Direct-to-Consumer Brands Sour on Facebook Ads." Digiday.com. https://digiday.com/marketing/pivot-traditional-direct-consumer-brands-sour-facebook-ads/. (Accessed January 26, 2020).

13. Liffreing, Ilyse. "Pivot to traditional: Direct-to-Consumer Brands Sour on Facebook Ads." Digiday.com. https://digiday.com/marketing/pivot-traditional-direct-consumer-brands-sour-facebook-ads/. (Accessed January 26, 2020).

14. Clifford, Catherine. "Social Media Guru: Facebook Video is the Best Ad Buy for Your Money Right Now." CNBC.com. https://www.cnbc.com/2017/03/17/social-media-guru-facebook-video-is-the-best-value-ad-buy-right-now.html. (Accessed January 26, 2020).

HIDDEN COSTS

15. Tribe Detroit. "Snap + Social + Solve." Tribedetroit.com. https://tribedetroit.com/snap-social-solve/. (accessed January 26, 2020).

EVERYTHING LOOKS THE SAME

16. Wu, Jasmine. "There are Now 175 Online Mattress Companies—and You Can't Tell Them Apart." CNBC.com. https://www.cnbc.com/2019/08/18/there-are-now-175-online-mattress-companiesand-you-cant-tell-them-apart.html. (accessed January 26, 2020).

17. Brunfaut, Thierry. Greenwood, Tom. "The Hottest Branding Trend of the Year is Also the Worst." Fastcompany.com. https://www.fastcompany.com/90276496/the-hottest-branding-trend-of-the-year-is-also-the-worst. (accessed January 26, 2020).

18. Wilson, Mark. "Why So Many Brands on Instagram Look the Same." Fastcompany.com. https://www.fastcompany.com/90281112/why-so-many-brands-on-instagram-look-the-same. (accessed January 26, 2020).

19. Odell, Amy. "Hiding 'Likes' is Good for the Influencer Economy." Businessoffashion.com. https://www.businessoffashion.com/articles/professional/how-hiding-likes-is-good-for-the-influencer-economy. (accessed January 26, 2020).

20. Hafer, Dylan. "You'll Die When You See Jessica Alba's Latest #spon Fail." Betches.com. https://betches.com/youll-die-when-you-see-jessica-albas-latest-spon-fail/. (accessed January 26, 2020).

THE VALUE OF FOLLOWERS

21. Jones, Allie. "What Happens When a Weddings Influencer Gets Divorced?" NYtimes.com. https://www.nytimes.com/2019/12/10/style/stone-fox-bride-molly-guy-divorce.html. (accessed January 26, 2020).

22. Social Blade. (2020). Stone Fox Ride's Instagram. https://socialblade.com/instagram/user/stonefoxride (accessed February 12, 2020).

23. Matsakis, Louise. "This Russian Vending Machine Will Sell You Fake Instagram Likes." Vice.com. https://www.vice.com/en_us/article/xw8yv3/russian-vending-machine-fake-instagram-likes. (accessed January 26, 2020).

24. Hafer, Dylan. "Are Those Obnoxious Kardashian Instagram Giveaways Fake? An Investigation." Betches.com. https://betches.com/are-those-obnoxious-kardashian-instagram-giveaways-fake-an-investigation/. (accessed January 26, 2020).

25. Hosie, Rachel. "An Instagram Star with 2 Million Followers Couldn't Sell 36 T-shirts, and a Marketing Expert Says Her Case isn't Rare." Insider.com. https://www.insider.com/instagrammer-arii-2-million-followers-cannot-sell-36-t-shirts-2019-5. (accessed January 26, 2020).

BUILDING YOUR HOUSE ON SOMEONE ELSE'S LAND

26. Carmen, Ashley. "When Facebook Goes Down, an Entire Economy Goes Down with It." TheVerge.com. https://www.theverge.com/2019/3/14/18265002/facebook-instagram-outage-ad-revenue-lost. (accessed January 26, 2020).

THE LANDLORD-TENANT RELATIONSHIP NOBODY WANTS

27. Greco, Alanna. "Dame Sex Toy Company's 'Eva' Hands-Free Couple's Vibrator Could Be a Game Changer." Bustle.com. https://www.bustle.com/articles/46437-dame-sex-toy-companys-eva-hands-free-couples-vibrator-could-be-a-game-changer. (accessed January 26, 2020).

28. Vu, Nancy. "These Women Are Suing to Let New York Subway Riders See Their Vibrators." Buzzfeednews.com. https://www.buzzfeednews.com/article/nancyvu/dame-sex-toy-company-sue-nyc-mta. (accessed January 26, 2020).

29. "Wikipedia: Free the Nipple (Campaign)." Wikimedia Foundation, last modified January 25, 2020. https://en.wikipedia.org/wiki/Free_the_Nipple_(campaign).

THE ICEBERG FILTER

30. Decker, Vivienne. "How Australia's Frank Body Built A $20 Million Global Beauty Brand on Social Media." Forbes.com. https://www.forbes.com/sites/viviennedecker/2017/02/22/how-australias-frank-body-built-a-20m-global-beauty-brand-on-social-media/#3a84d6814709. (accessed January 26, 2020).

31. Richards, Kate. "How Stoney Clover Lane Marries DTC and Physical Stores." Glossy.com. https://www.glossy.co/fashion/how-stoney-clover-lane-marries-dtc-and-physical-stores. (accessed January 26, 2020).

STRATEGIC DIVERSIFICATION

32. Hogan, Cara. "The Empowered Marketer: Maurice Tebele and Martin Hoffstein of JAJA Tequila." Zaius.com. https://www.zaius.com/learn/the-empowered-marketer-jaja-tequila/. (accessed January 26, 2020).

GO WHERE YOUR CUSTOMERS ARE

33. Ross, Harling. "Inside the Endearing Cult of Susan Alexandra." Manrepeller.com. https://www.manrepeller.com/2019/09/the-cult-of-susan-alexandra.html. (accessed January 26, 2020).

34. Scheffler, Daniel. "Detroit Upstart Floyd Wants to Change How We Furnish Our Homes." Curbed.com. https://www.curbed.com/2016/7/19/12197656/floyd-detroit-furniture-modular-diy. (accessed January 26, 2020).

35. Scheffler, Daniel. "Detroit Upstart Floyd Wants to Change How We Furnish Our Homes." Curbed.com.
https://www.curbed.com/2016/7/19/12197656/floyd-detroit-furniture-modular-diy. (accessed January 26, 2020).

36. Chen, Jenn. "Important Instagram Stats You Need to Know for 2020." Sproutsocial.com.
https://sproutsocial.com/insights/instagram-stats/. (accessed January 26, 2020).

37. Keller, Hadley. "A New Way to Discover Furniture? In Your Airbnb." Architecturaldigest.com.
https://www.architecturaldigest.com/story/a-new-way-to-discover-furniture-in-your-airbnb.(accessed January 26, 2020).

YOU'VE GOTTA HAVE A GIMMICK

38. Hiebert, Paul. "This CBD Brand Found a Workaround to Instagram's Cannabis Promotion Rules." Adweek.com
https://www.adweek.com/brand-marketing/this-cbd-brand-paid-people-3-via-venmo-to-promote-its-post/. (accessed January 26, 2020).

39. Murphy, Brandon. "Harnessing the Power of Consumer Advocacy to Fuel Effective Growth." Deloitte.
https://www.slideshare.net/brandonmurphy/brand-advocacy-and-social-media-2009-gma-conference. (accessed January 26, 2020).

GOING WHOLESALE

40. Smith, Craig. "45 Interesting Facts About Target." Expandedramblings.com.
https://expandedramblings.com/index.php/target-statistics/.
(accessed January 26, 2020).

41. Richards, Katie. "Built on Instagram, Adina's Jewels is Looking to Department Stores for New Customers." Glossy.co.
https://www.glossy.co/fashion/built-on-instagram-adinas-jewels-is-looking-to-department-stores-for-new-customers. (accessed January 26, 2020).

42."Bulletin FAQ," Bulletin Brands.
https://bulletin.co/faq/meet-bulletin. (accessed January 26, 2020).

43. Milnes, Hilary. "'A Giant Billboard for the Company': How Digitally Native Brands are Navigating Wholesale Partnerships." Digiday.com.
https://digiday.com/marketing/giant-billboard-company-digitally-native-brands-negotiate-wholesale-partnerships/. (accessed January 26, 2020).

44. Milnes, Hilary. "How Nordstrom Changed its Merchandising Strategy for the DTC Brand Era." Glossy.co.
https://www.glossy.co/fashion/how-nordstrom-changed-its-merchandising-strategy-for-the-dtc-brand-era. (accessed January 26, 2020).

THE ROAD TO RETAIL

45. Fara, Emily. "La Ligne's First Store is Opening Today on Madison Avenue." Vogue.com. https://www.vogue.com/article/la-ligne-first-store-new-york. (accessed January 26, 2020).

46. Arsenault, Bridget. "Inside Hill House Home: A New Female-Founded Brand Shaking Up the Retail Industry." Forbes.com. https://www.forbes.com/sites/bridgetarsenault/2019/11/18/inside-hill-house-home-a-new-female-founded-brand-shaking-up-the-retail-industry/#27ed26085b77. (accessed January 26, 2020).

47. Cantrell, Liz. "Lingua Franca opens its first retail store." Townandcountrymag.com. https://www.townandcountrymag.com/style/fashion-trends/a25008888/lingua-franca-first-retail-store-new-york-city/. (accessed January 26, 2020).

48. Richards, Katie. "How Naadam is Subtracting Risk from its Physical Retail Expansion." Glossy.co. https://www.glossy.co/fashion/how-naadam-is-subtracting-risk-from-its-physical-retail-expansion. (accessed January 26, 2020).

CONCLUSION

49. Fleming, Olivia. "Why the World's Most Talked About Art Dealer is Instagram." Vogue.com. https://www.vogue.com/article/buying-and-selling-art-on-instagram. (accessed January 26, 2020).

ACKNOWLEDGEMENTS

Larry, thank you for pushing me to get out of bed and work my hardest even on our toughest days. You encouraged me to write this book and to finish this book, and for that I cannot thank you enough. You read and reread every single sentence, you added words I'd never heard of before and increased my syllable count 5-fold just because. This process gave me a glimpse into how tedious homework time will be with our kids and to be quite honest, I am scared. I'm so lucky to have you and your two Ivy League degrees supporting me no matter what project I decide to take on. You love me so much, and it shows.

Mom and Dad, thank you for letting me live at home without so much as lifting a finger around the house while pregnant and writing this book (except maybe one or two times).

Hannah, Marc and Claire, thank you for understanding that I was actually writing this thing when I was sitting on the couch in the kitchen all day, every day.

Missy, what a year, or has it been two years? Glad we made it through. I couldn't have done it without you.

Aunt Julie and Uncle Eric, thank you for convincing me to finish this book when we were eating French onion soup in Paris and I was ready to quit.

Thank you to The Wharton School, which I did not actually attend. I miss you and Philadelphia every single day.

And finally, thank you to everyone who took time out of their schedules to sit with me and talk about my love-hate relationship with my favorite addiction, Instagram.